BUILD IT TOGETHER

BUILD IT TOGETHER

Twenty-seven
Easy-to-make
Woodworking
Projects for
Adults and
Children

by
Katie and Gene Hamilton

CHARLES SCRIBNER'S SONS NEW YORK

To our mothers

Copyright © 1983, 1984 Katie and Gene Hamilton

Library of Congress Cataloging in Publication Data

Hamilton, Katie.
  Build it together.

  1. Woodwork.   I. Hamilton, Gene.   II. Title.
TT185.H318   1984   684'.08   84-1254
  ISBN 0-684-18093-6 (cloth)
  ISBN 0-684-18092-8 (pbk.)

This book published simultaneously
in the United States of America and in Canada—
Copyright under the Berne Convention.

Q   C.)

1 3 5 7 9 11 13 15 17 19   Q/C   20 18 16 14 12 10 8 6 4 2

1 3 5 7 9 11 13 15 17 19   Q/P   20 18 16 14 12 10 8 6 4 2

Printed in the United States of America.

Acknowledgments

We'd like to thank all the parents and kids who participated in producing our book. Without them, we couldn't have done it. Our sincere thanks go to Jodi and Matt Arndt, David Backhaus, John Bolsinger, Scott Broman, Judith Cookis, Alana and Tony Eaton, Jodi Foris, Adam Gohr, Scott Greiwe, Brian Hamilton, Sean Hamilton, Paul Jacobsen, Katie and Sally Keigher, Tommy Kelly, Amy and Michael Nolfo, Genevieve Pazdan, Lauren and Robin Quinn, Caryn Tahl, Joanna Wolaver, Michael Wolgemuth, Elizabeth and Mark Van Doren, Ellen Zipprich, and their moms, dads, and grandfathers.

Special thanks to dear friends Kay and Len Hilts, who have fostered our careers and coached us kindly along the way.

And last, but certainly not least, we are sincerely grateful to our agent, Jane Jordan Browne, and our editor, Maron L. Waxman, who helped us launch this, our first book, off the idea board and into reality.

Contents

Introduction

Welcome to our workshop and the world of woodworking.

Here we've designed simple-to-make woodworking projects for an adult and child to build together. It's rewarding to make something from a piece of wood, and the satisfaction of doing it with someone special makes it even more fun.

All the 27 projects in this book are designed for beginners, people with little or no experience in woodworking. You don't need a fancy workshop and expensive power tools. Our projects can be built with hand tools on a kitchen or Ping-Pong table. The materials are easy-to-find dimensional lumber available at home centers and lumberyards.

For each project we have estimated the amount of time you can expect to spend building it and have provided a shopping list for materials, And, of course, we caution you about safety while working with wood. Always wear a pair of inexpensive safety glasses or goggles to protect your eyes when using a striking or cutting tool like a hammer or a saw.

During construction you are guided step by step and can refer to an accurate cutting list for each project. It gives the exact size of each piece of wood. An important point to remember about dimensional lumber is that the nominal size is not its actual size. For example, a 1″ × 3″ piece of lumber listed in the shopping list actually measures only ¾″ × 2½″. Wood is measured before it is milled smooth and dried, which reduces its overall thickness by about ½ inch. Our cutting lists give actual measurements.

Along with the "nuts and bolts" information there are step-by-step pictures that illustrate the building of each project and a set of plans showing how it all goes together. Although the projects are easy to build, you should read the instructions and carefully look over the pictures before starting any project. Apprentice woodworkers quickly learn it pays to measure twice and cut once.

We parent-and-kid-tested each design on our friends, neighbors, and relatives, who acted as models. Sometimes they helped us with the idea for a project or the design itself.

It was a team effort all the way, and that's what this book is about. We hope kids and their parents or grandparents, teachers or scout leaders, find projects they want to build and then get right to it and enjoy the wonderful fun of building together.

Hanging Plant Holder

TIME REQUIRED: half day (time needed for cutting, building, and assembling project; does not include drying time of glue or finish)

Carpenters use parting stop—pine molding—to make windows, but you can use it to make a hanging plant holder. Parting stop is readily available at lumberyards and home centers. It comes in long, narrow pieces, easy to cut and glue together.

Our ribbed basket makes an attractive holder for any plant that needs space to stretch out and grow. It's held up with strong natural jute twine.

You build the frame like a log cabin. It's so easy that very little help is needed from the older member of your carpentry team. The dimensions of our holder are suitable for a 4″ pot and tray, but construction is simple enough for you to design it to fit whatever size pot you have.

If your lumberyard doesn't stock parting stop, buy an 8′ number 2 pine one-by-four and have the yardman rip off three ½″-thick strips. He might charge a small fee for this service.

Take a look at the parting stop, and you'll see that it's not square. When you're gluing and nailing ribs together, put glue on the ½″ side of all ribs. You'll also find that it's easier to drive nails into the ribs before you place them in position. This makes alignment easy and prevents damage to lower ribs from excessive hammering.

You can save time and have a better-looking stain job if you apply the stain before assembly. Other finishes, like paint, should be applied after the holder is tightly glued together.

Construction of your plant holder begins by cutting the parting stop to length. An inexpensive wooden miter box will help you make square cuts at the ends and improve the appearance of your holder, but it's not required. Use a ruler to mark the length of each set of ribs, and cut them to size, following the Cutting List.

The planter is assembled upside down. Begin with the longest set of ribs (A), and lay them parallel to each other about 10″ apart. Take the second set (B), and drive a number 3 finishing nail through the center of the ribs about 1½″ from each end. Turn the rib over, and apply a small amount of glue around the area where the nail point comes out. Place the second set of ribs on top of the first

1

set, aligning them so the nail is centered and the ends overlap evenly. Hammer the nails in, then repeat this process on the other side.

Check to see whether the first two sets of ribs are square by placing a square against one corner. Any piece of cardboard that has a square corner can also be used.

The next layer of ribs, the third, is applied the same way. Locate the nail position by placing the third set of ribs on the second, align it, and mark the position of the nail on both ends. Remove the rib, and drive nails through the mark until their points just stick out. Do the same to the other ribs in the third set, putting a drop of glue on the spot where the nail point comes out, and then nail both in place.

As the holder takes shape, check to see that it's square. Sight down one side to make sure it's not twisted.

The last layer (this is the bottom) is made from the six ribs in the tenth set. Before nailing on the two outside bottom ribs, drill a $\frac{3}{16}''$ hole about $\frac{1}{2}''$ from the ends of these ribs for the hanging twine to pass through. Then arrange these ribs so their spacing is equal across the holder's bottom.

Cut two pieces of jute or heavy twine twice the distance from the plant holder to its hanging hook. Pass the jute through one hole you drilled in the bottom rib, and tie a knot in its end so it can't slip out. Pass the other end through the hole at the opposite end, and knot it. Repeat this for the other side.

Of course, you can use rawhide shoelaces, macraméd twine, rope, wire, cord, and beads to suspend the plant holder.

Finish your holder with a coat of polyurethane varnish, or paint it.

Secure the holder to the ceiling with an adequate anchor. Remember plants are heavy; use a heavy-duty plastic plaster anchor or an expansion-type anchor rated for fifty pounds or more.

SHOPPING LIST

Item	Quantity
$\frac{3}{4}'' \times \frac{1}{2}'' \times 8'$ pine parting stop	3
number 3 finishing nails	1 box
carpenter's glue	6-ounce bottle
heavy twine	1 ball
plastic plant pot	1

CUTTING LIST

Part	Name	Quantity	Size	Material
A	first rib	2	$\frac{3}{4}'' \times \frac{1}{2}'' \times 13''$	pine
B	second rib	2	$\frac{3}{4}'' \times \frac{1}{2}'' \times 12\frac{1}{2}''$	pine
C	third rib	2	$\frac{3}{4}'' \times \frac{1}{2}'' \times 12''$	pine
D	fourth rib	2	$\frac{3}{4}'' \times \frac{1}{2}'' \times 11\frac{1}{2}''$	pine
E	fifth rib	2	$\frac{3}{4}'' \times \frac{1}{2}'' \times 11''$	pine
F	sixth rib	2	$\frac{3}{4}'' \times \frac{1}{2}'' \times 10\frac{1}{2}''$	pine
G	seventh rib	2	$\frac{3}{4}'' \times \frac{1}{2}'' \times 10''$	pine
H	eighth rib	2	$\frac{3}{4}'' \times \frac{1}{2}'' \times 9\frac{1}{2}''$	pine
I	ninth rib	2	$\frac{3}{4}'' \times \frac{1}{2}'' \times 9''$	pine
J	tenth rib	6	$\frac{3}{4}'' \times \frac{1}{2}'' \times 7''$	pine

An inexpensive wooden miter box guarantees square ends.

Measure 1½″ from the end of the second rib, and mark location for the nail on the ½″ side.

Drive number 3 finishing nails through the rib until its point is just coming out the back.

Place a drop of glue on the rib where the nail point comes out.

Nail the rib in place after making sure that the ends overlap equally on both sides.

Use a square to check the corners of the first layer of ribs.

Mark the location of a nail on the ribs by placing it in position and making a pencil mark at the spot where the nail will pass through both ribs.

Clamp one of the outside ribs of the tenth set to your table, and drill a ³⁄₁₆" hole in both of its ends for the hanging twine. Repeat for other outside rib.

Pass heavy twine through the holes, and tie a knot at its end.

Finished hanging plant holder.

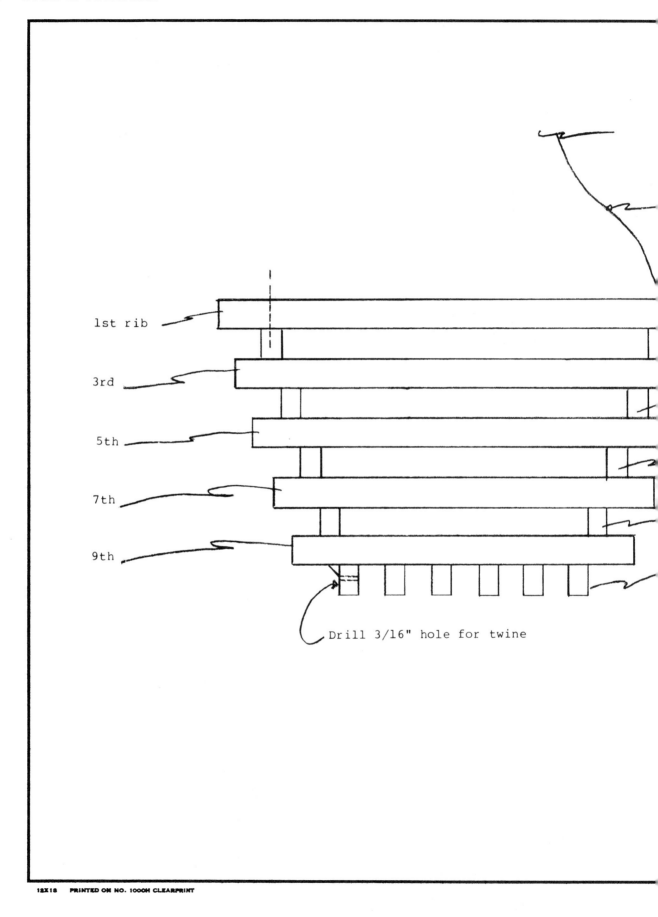

1st rib

3rd

5th

7th

9th

Drill 3/16" hole for twine

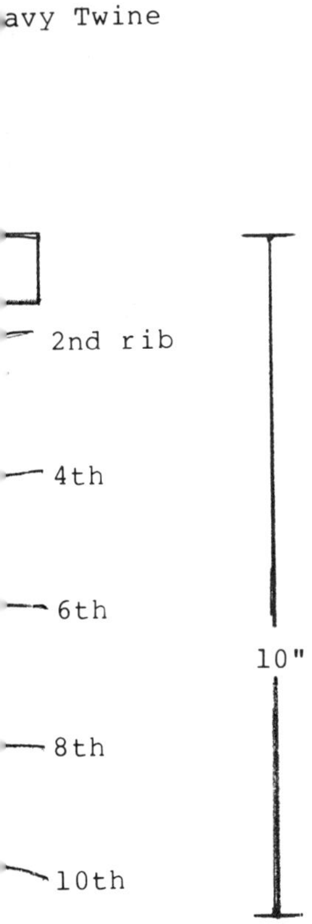

avy Twine

2nd rib

4th

6th

10"

8th

10th

	Hanging Plant Holder		
	APPROVED BY:		**DRAWN BY** *GH*
DATE: 1/6/83			**REVISED**
	BUILD IT TOGETHER		
	Gene and Katie Hamilton		**DRAWING NUMBER** 2/1

Big and Little Tool Boxes

TIME REQUIRED: half day for each (time needed for cutting, building, and assembling project; does not include drying time of glue or finish)

Not too long ago, the first project most apprentices completed was a box to hold their tools. Here are two easy-to-construct traditional tool boxes, one scaled for a master craftsman, the other just right for his apprentice.

These matching tool boxes are constructed out of inexpensive but hardworking pine with hardboard bottoms. There is room for long-handled tools such as hammers and saws, plus small items like nails and measuring tape. Your screwdrivers and chisels are stored in custom-made compartments that hold them in a handy upright position.

Our boxes are sized to be built with standard dimensional lumber, with no long ripsaw cuts required. Since construction of both tool boxes is identical except for the dimensions, we will concentrate on the apprentice box.

Begin by laying out the dimensions of the ends (A), sides (B), nail-compartment partitions (D), and divider (E) on the wood (see Cutting List). Use a combination square to draw straight layout lines. Securely clamp the wood to a table, or place it in a vise for safe and accurate cutting. When cutting, keep your saw to the waste side of the layout lines. Don't forget to wear safety glasses whenever you use cutting or striking tools.

The sloping end shoulders of part A are laid out by making a full-sized cardboard pattern (see plan) and then tracing it on the face of the end. When you clamp part A for cutting, place a piece of scrap wood along the layout line to guide the saw.

The handle slot in the divider (E) is next on the list. Make a mark for the slot holes 6½" from the ends and 1¼" from the top edge. Through these spots, drill 1" holes to form the outside corners of the handle. Use a keyhole or coping saw to make straight cuts from hole edge to hole edge. Sand the handle cutout smooth with a piece of number 120 sandpaper wrapped around a short piece of dowel.

After you've finished cutting all the parts, sand them with number 120 grit sandpaper. Then test fit the parts, and correct any bad fits before assembly. If everything fits, your tool box is ready to glue up.

Make a light pencil mark down the center of the ends to help you keep nails straight. Drive number 4 finishing nails placed about 1½″ apart along this line. Then run a bead of carpenter's glue down the end of the divider, and align it in the center of the end (A). Check that the divider is flush with the bottom of side B, and then nail it in place. Do the same at other end.

Before you glue on the sides, install nail compartments (D). Use glue and number 4 finishing nails. Then nail and glue on the sides. Your tool box is ready for its bottom.

The bottom (C) is held in place with 1″ roofing nails placed about 1½″ apart. Drill ⅛″ pilot holes for these nails, then apply glue and nail the bottom in place.

Your new tool box is ready for finishing. We liked the natural pine look, but you can finish your box with paint or stain.

After the finish has dried, you can customize your tool box to meet your exact needs by making tool holders out of heavy shoelaces held in place with tacks or staples. All you have to do is lay the tool in place, put the shoelace in position over the tool blade, and tack it down. Keep the shoelace snug but not too tight so that the tool will be easy to insert.

Now that your apprentice has completed his own tool box, he'll be ready to tackle the larger box; he might not even need the master to help on this one.

SHOPPING LIST

Item	Quantity
7½″ × 72″ × ¾″ pine (1″ × 8″)	2
3½″ × 72″ × ¾″ pine (1″ × 4″)	2
24″ × 48″ × ¼″ hardboard (quarter sheet)	1
number 4 finishing nails	1 box
1″ roofing nails	1 box
¾″ tacks	1 box
heavy shoelaces	2 laces
carpenter's glue	6-ounce bottle
finish	1 quart

CUTTING LIST
Large Box

Part	Name	Quantity	Size	Material
A	end	2	7½″ × 7½″ × ¾″	pine
B	side	2	3½″ × 24″ × ¾″	pine
C	bottom	1	9″ × 24″ × ¼″	hardboard
D	nail compartment	2	3½″ × 3⅜″ × ¾″	pine
E	divider	1	7½″ × 22½″ × ¾″	pine

CUTTING LIST
Small Box

Part	Name	Quantity	Size	Material
A	end	2	7½″ × 7½″ × ¾″	pine
B	side	2	3½″ × 18″ × ¾″	pine
C	bottom	1	9″ × 18″ × ¼″	hardboard
D	nail compartment	2	3½″ × 3⅜″ × ¾″	pine
E	divider	1	7″ × 16½″ × ¾″	pine

Lay out the length of the pieces with a ruler and combination square for straight cut lines.

When cutting stock to length, make all saw cuts to the waste side of layout lines.

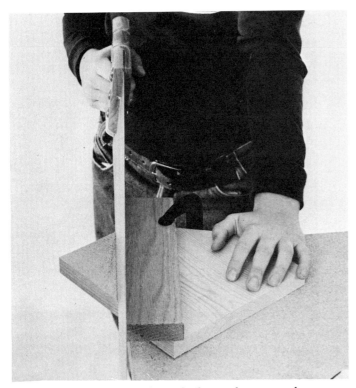

Clamp a piece of scrap along the layout line to guide the saw when cutting the ends.

Mark the location of the handle slot holes 6½″ from the ends and 1¼″ from the top of the divider (E).

Clamp divider securely, and use a brace and bit to bore two 1″ holes for the handle slot.

Cut from hole edge to hole edge with a keyhole saw or coping saw.

When nailing the ends (A) to the divider (E), have one carpenter keep pieces in alignment while the other drives the nails.

Glue and nail on sides (B) with number 4 finishing nails.

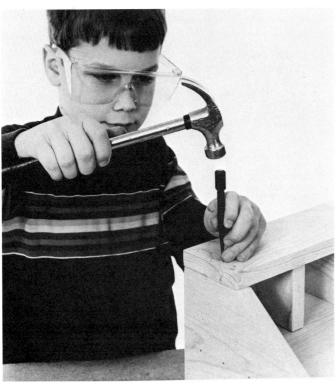

Use a nail set to sink nailheads below the wood's
surface.

Apply glue to the bottom frame, and after
predrilling nail holes in the hardboard
bottom (C), attach bottom with 1″
galvanized roofing nails.

When the bottom is attached, you can give your tool
box the finish of your choice.

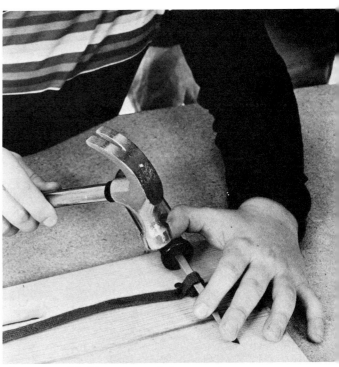

Custom tool holders are made by stretching a
heavy shoelace over the tool and tacking it
in place.

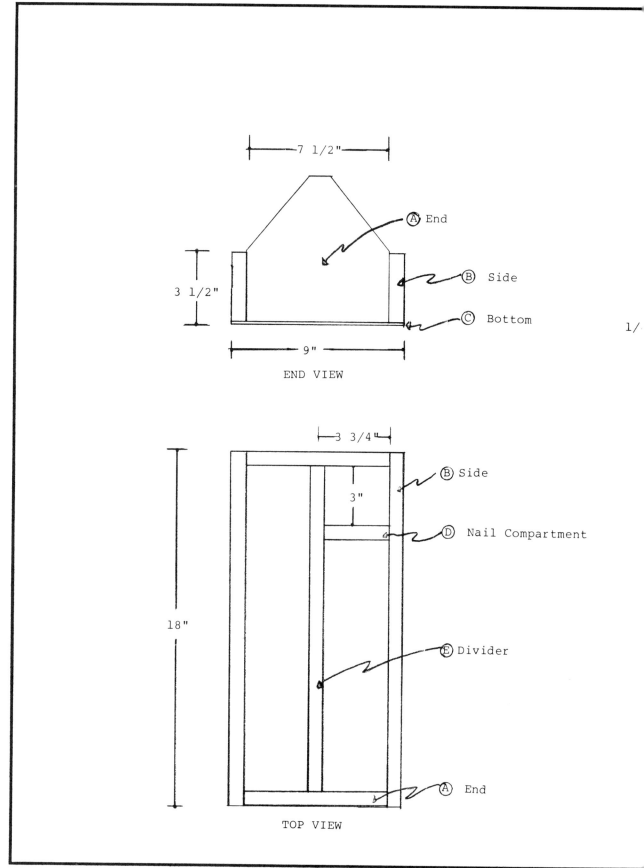

7 1/2"

Ⓐ End

3 1/2"

Ⓑ Side

Ⓒ Bottom

9"

END VIEW

3 3/4"

Ⓑ Side

3"

Ⓓ Nail Compartment

18"

Ⓔ Divider

Ⓐ End

TOP VIEW

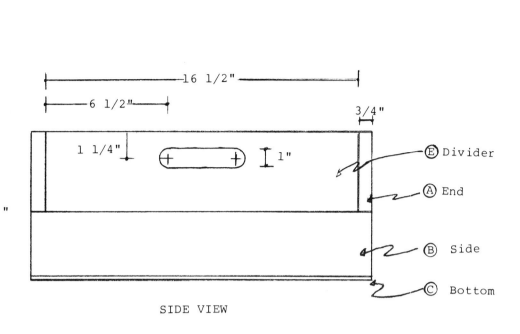

SIDE VIEW

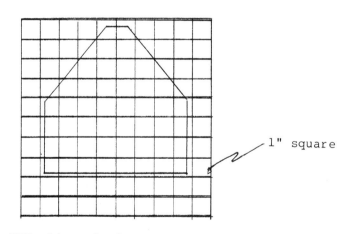

END Big and Little Tool Box

		Big and Little Tool Boxes	
	APPROVED BY:		**DRAWN BY**
DATE: 1/7/83			**REVISED**
	BUILD IT TOGETHER		
	Katie and Gene Hamilton		**DRAWING NUMBER** 3/1

Ball and Bat Rack

TIME REQUIRED: half day (time needed for cutting, building, and assembling project; does not include drying time of glue or finish)

What better place to stow baseball equipment than in this simple-to-build ball and bat rack? Any little leaguer can proudly display his or her favorite baseball gear *and* keep it neatly stored and out of the way. Our rack is designed for two bats and three balls, with pegs for gloves, batting helmets, or caps. It can be expanded to hold enough for a whole team and customized to fit bats and balls.

The rack is cut from 1″ × 4″ pine stock, readily available at local lumberyards and home centers. All you have to do is cut wood to length. An inexpensive wooden miter box will help small hands make square cuts, but it's not necessary.

Begin construction by laying out the bottom (A), back (B), and top (C) on 1″ × 4″ stock (see Cutting List). Then cut each piece.

Three holes are drilled in the top piece to hold the baseballs. The centers of these holes are located 1½″ from the front edge and 2½″ from each

end and in the center of the top. Mark these points, and bore a 2″ hole through them for the baseballs to sit in.

Lay out the two bat slots in the same way. Their center holes are located 1½″ from the front edge of the bottom and 3″ from each end. Drill 1½″ holes through the layout marks for bat slots.

An electric drill and hole cutter will make quick work of cutting out these large holes, but this is best left to the older carpenter. If you use a brace and expandable bit, securely clamp parts to the table, and either carpenter can drill away.

Use a combination square to draw straight lines from the edges of the bat slot holes to the front edge of the bottom. Use a saw, and cut inside these lines to form slots for the bat handles.

Sand the pieces with number 120 grit paper. Round off all corners in the bat slots and baseball holes by wrapping sandpaper around a dowel.

Assembly is easy. Begin by driving four evenly spaced number 4 finishing nails along the back edges of the top and bottom. Drive them through the pieces until just the tip protrudes from the other side.

Next have one team member run a bead of

glue down the top edge of the back. Then, while one member holds the back straight to keep edges in alignment, the other nails on the top. Now turn the rack over, and glue and nail the bottom to the back.

For the glove and hat pegs, drill two ⅜″ holes in the front edge of the bottom piece 1″ from each end. Drill this hole at an upward angle to prevent your hat and glove from slipping off. Use an adjustable bevel set at a slight angle (5 degrees) to act as a guide. If you don't have a bevel, cut a piece of cardboard to a 5-degree angle, and use it as a guide.

Turn your rack on its back, and put a drop of glue in the dowel holes and tap in ⅜″ dowels (D). Set the whole works aside for the glue to dry.

When the glue is dry, use a nail set to sink the heads of the finishing nails below the wood surface. Scrape off the excess glue with a chisel, and give the rack a final sanding; it's ready to stain, paint, or varnish.

You can attach your rack to a wall with plastic wall anchors. If you have enlarged its capacity, use expansion-type fasteners. We used large picture-hanging brackets and finishing nails driven into the lath of a plaster wall. If your walls are covered with drywall, use plastic wall anchors. Tighten the anchor screws until their heads are ⅛″ from the wall surface, then hook the picture brackets over the screw heads.

SHOPPING LIST

Item	Quantity
1″ × 4″ number 2 pine	4′
⅜″ hardwood dowel	6″
number 4 finishing nails	small box
carpenter's glue	6-ounce bottle
number 120 sandpaper	1 sheet
stain, paint, or finish	1 pint

CUTTING LIST

Part	Name	Quantity	Size	Material
A	bottom	1	3½″ × 12″ × ¾″	1″ × 4″ pine
B	back	1	3½″ × 12″ × ¾″	1″ × 4″ pine
C	top	1	3½″ × 12″ × ¾″	1″ × 4″ pine
D	peg	2	2½″ × ⅜″	⅜″ hardwood dowel

Use a tape and combination square to lay out the cutting lines.

Mark the location of the centers of the bat holes 3″ from the end and 1½″ in from the front edge.

With a brace and bit or power hand drill and hole cutter, bore a 1½″ hole through these layout marks for the bat slot.

Draw straight lines from the edge of the bat slot holes to the front edge.

Cut inside layout lines to form the bat slots.

Give all pieces a sanding with number 120 paper, and predrive 4 evenly spaced number 4 finishing nails along the back edges of the top and bottom.

Apply glue to the top of the back.

Align the top with the back, and drive in the nails until their heads are almost flush with the wood surface.

After glue has dried, use a nail set to sink nailheads slightly below the wood surface.

Finished ball and bat rack.

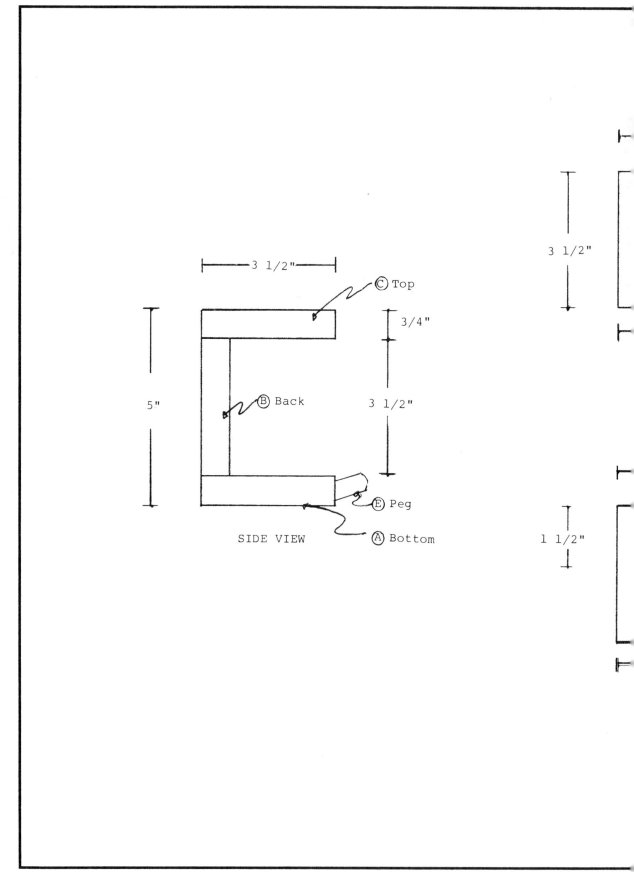

3 1/2"

© Top

3/4"

5"

® Back

3 1/2"

© Peg

SIDE VIEW

Ⓐ Bottom

3 1/2"

1 1/2"

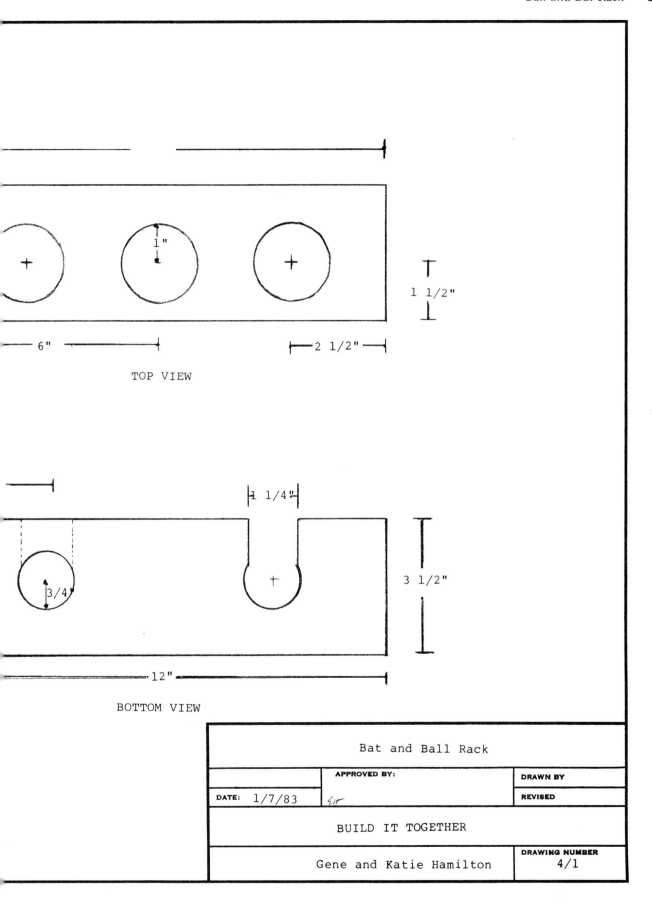

TOP VIEW

1"

1 1/2"

6"

2 1/2"

1 1/4"

3 1/2"

3/4

12"

BOTTOM VIEW

		Bat and Ball Rack		
	APPROVED BY:		DRAWN BY	
DATE: 1/7/83			REVISED	
		BUILD IT TOGETHER		
		Gene and Katie Hamilton	DRAWING NUMBER 4/1	

$\mathbb{K}$*nife Block*

TIME REQUIRED: half day (time needed for cutting, building, and assembling project; does not include drying time of glue or finish)

Even the best knives will lose their edges if not stored properly. Our knife block gives knives protection and makes a wonderful gift. It looks expensive but isn't because our design is simple and we used pine instead of maple. This block is sure to put a smile on the face of any chef and will handsomely grace the fanciest of kitchens.

Since our block is made of layers of common 1″ × 8″ pine boards and ¼″ lattice glued together, the materials are inexpensive. Except for cutting, all the work can be tackled by an inexperienced apprentice.

The block is 10½″ high, 5¾″ wide, and 7½″ long. It was designed to hold five knives and a sharpening steel, but you can design your knife block to hold more or fewer knives.

All lumberyards stock number 2 1″ × 8″ pine. When shopping for materials, select boards that are flat and knot-free along their edges. Knots in the center of boards are all right since the interior laminates are hidden. If your lumberyard doesn't stock lattice 3¾″ wide, purchase what is available. You can glue several pieces edge to edge to make the 7½″ width. Please note that you can't have the pieces cut at the lumberyard; they have to be cut after the block is partially assembled.

Measure your knives before you begin cutting; a height of 10½″ will house most knives. If you have a large chef's or bread knife, change the height of the block to fit it.

Begin construction by gluing the ¼″ lattice together edge to edge to form a piece 7½″ wide. Cut the narrow lattice into pieces 24″ long. Glue these pieces edge to edge to make parts 7½″ wide and 24″ long. This saves gluing time because you form two parts at a time. After the glue is dry, cut these pieces in half to form both B parts.

Gluing the lattice together is easy. Apply glue to the edges of the pieces, and then place four rubber bands around them. Put them on wax paper or aluminum foil, and place a heavy object on top of them. You can stack both assemblies on top of each other to dry, but insert wax paper or foil between the pieces.

While the glue is drying, cut the thick laminate pieces (A) from the 1″ × 8″ stock. Use a combination square to draw straight cut lines across the board, and keep your saw cuts to the waste side of this line.

After the thin pieces have dried, cut them into five equal pieces 10½″ inches long. The cutouts for the knives are laid out next. Decide the order in which you want the knives to be arranged in the block, numbering each one. Then lay a knife on piece B, and trace around the blade. Do this for all the knives. After tracing all the knives, number the laminate parts so they can be assembled in the right order come gluing time.

Remove the wood inside the knife-blade outlines with a coping saw. A saber or jigsaw can also be used. Securely clamp the pieces to the table, or place them in a vise. Have one member support the wood while the other makes cutouts for the large knives. Don't worry if the piece breaks at the bottom, since it will be glued between two thick pieces of pine.

Gluing up the block is easy but messy. Protect your table with plenty of paper. Begin by selecting a knot-free thick piece for the outside. Place it on the table with its better side facing down. Take the first thin piece with knife-blade cutouts, and smear plenty of glue on the side that will be glued to the thick piece. Put it in place, sliding it around to spread the glue. Then spread the glue on its other side, and place the second thick piece over it, again sliding the piece around to spread the glue.

To keep the sandwich in alignment when you are clamping, drive several number 3 finishing nails through the pieces. One team member should hold the pieces in alignment when the other is nailing. Do this after the second thick piece is in place and to each layer thereafter. Don't nail the last laminate piece in place, because the nails will show.

You now have a gluey mess. For best results, clamp the laminates together with four bar clamps, making sure the outside laminate pieces are in alignment. Use scrap pieces under the clamp jaws to prevent marring the sides. If you don't have clamps, place the block on its side, and put something heavy on top of it.

After the glue has dried, the block must be sanded smooth. Use an electric hand drill equipped with an inexpensive sanding disk. The older carpenter should take charge of grinding the block. The apprentice can finish the sanding by hand or with an orbital sander.

Fill any slight gaps with wood putty, and sand them smooth. Then wipe the dust off, and apply several coats of mineral oil.

Note: Do not use a toxic finish on wood surfaces that will come in contact with food.

SHOPPING LIST

Item	Quantity
1″ × 8″ number 2 pine	8′
¼″ × 3¾″ pine lattice	8′
carpenter's glue	6-ounce bottle
number 3 finishing nails	small box
number 100 grit sanding disk	3 disks
number 120 grit sandpaper	1 sheet
mineral oil	1 pint

CUTTING LIST

Part	Name	Quantity	Size	Material
A	thick piece	6	7½″ × 10½″ × ¾″	1″ × 8″ pine
B	thin piece	5	7½″ × 10½″ × ¼″	¼″ pine lattice

Note: The cutting for this project cannot be done at the lumberyard. It must be done during construction of the project.

Mark the length of the thick (A) and thin
(B) laminate parts on the wood stock.

Clamp parts securely to the table, then cut
to length.

*Trace the shape of the knife blades on the
thin laminate (B).*

*Cut out the knife-blade patterns from the thin
laminate. Support the piece well when cutting.*

Apply glue to the thin laminate and position it on the thick part.

Drive several number 3 finishing nails through the laminate to prevent shifting during clamping.

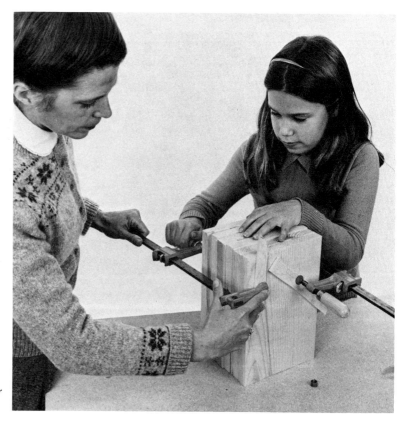

Apply clamps using scraps under the jaws to protect the block.

Grind smooth irregular spots with an electric hand drill equipped with a sanding disk.

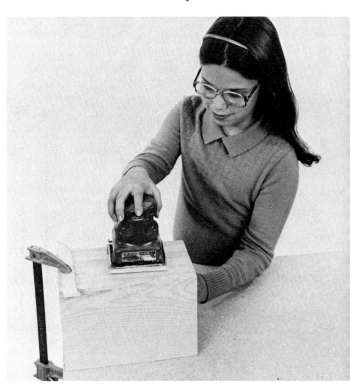

Finish the block by sanding with an orbital sander or a hand sanding block.

Finished knife block.

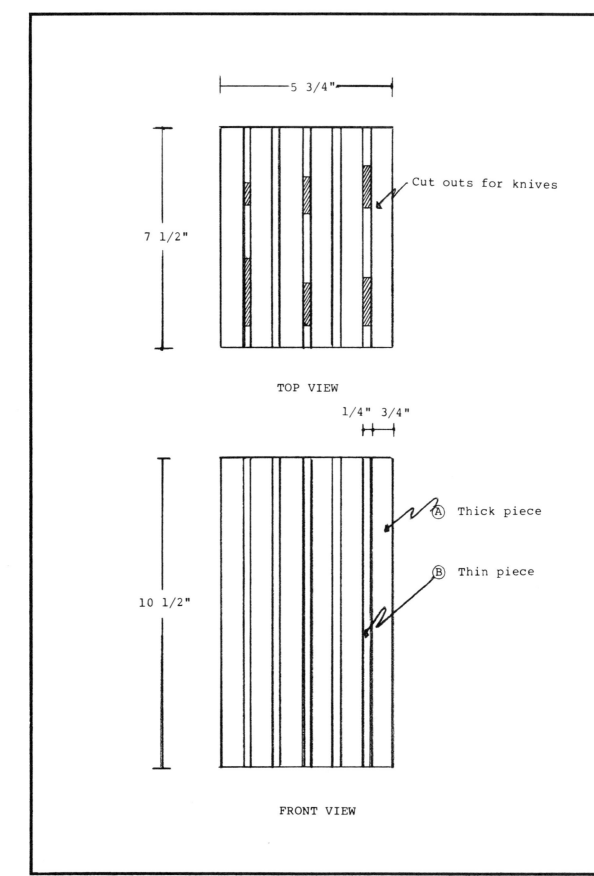

TOP VIEW

FRONT VIEW

Trace shape of knife blade on to piece of wood.
Cut out using coping saw.

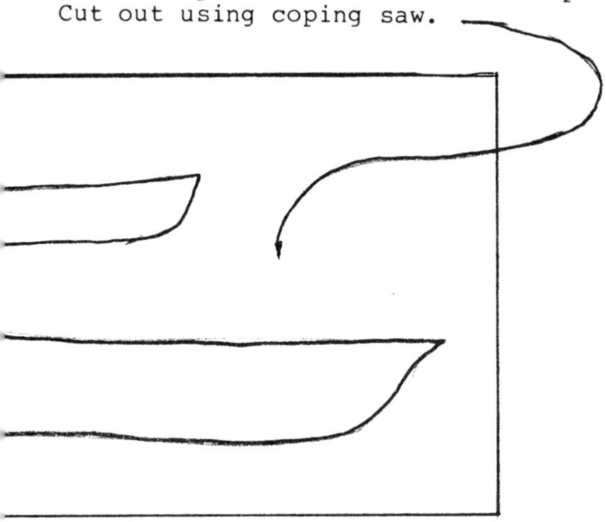

SIDE VIEW

Thin Piece

	Knife Block		
	APPROVED BY:		**DRAWN BY** _GH_
DATE: 1/7/83	_GH_		**REVISED**
	BUILD IT TOGETHER		
	Katie and Gene Hamilton		**DRAWING NUMBER** 5/1

Kitchen Trivet

TIME REQUIRED: almost instant (two to three hours; time needed for cutting, building, and assembling project; does not include drying time of glue or finish)

Our kitchen trivet is not only a useful gift; it's easy to make. This almost instant project is constructed around an inexpensive 8″-square ceramic tile with scraps of lumber for its sides. Since there is little cutting for the carpenters to do, this might be a good beginning project for inexperienced parents or young woodworkers to tackle.

Our trivet measures 8½″ square, but you can make a larger hotplate using several tiles, either two or three in a row to form a rectangle or four to make a large square. The tile you choose can be colorfully painted or glazed a single color. The selection of tiles is endless, so look for ones that match your kitchen, dishes, or table.

The tile sits on a piece of square flakeboard and rests on feet made of furniture tack glides. We chose maple for the sides, but inexpensive pine lattice is easier to find and can be substituted.

Begin by laying out the bottom (A) on the piece of flakeboard or plywood. To do this, measure out an 8″ square, marking the corners. Then connect these marks with straight lines to form the square. Cut along the lines, keeping your saw to the waste side.

To cut the sides (B and C), clamp the lattice or maple piece to the table. Support the end for a square cut. An inexpensive miter box helps with these cuts but is not necessary. Measure and cut the two short side pieces (B) to a length of 8″. The long sides (C) are cut to 8½″.

You will find it easier to predrive the nails into the side pieces before they are glued to the edge of the bottom piece. Space four number 3 finishing nails 2″ from each end and about ¼″ from the bottom of the pieces B and C. If you use maple for the sides, nailing will be easier if you drill ⅟₁₆″ pilot holes.

Run a bead of glue along one edge of the bottom, and glue a short side to it. Position the side piece so it is flush with the bottom and aligns at the end. Drive the nails into the bottom. Now repeat on the opposite side of the bottom for the other short side.

Glue the long sides (C) to the bottom in same way. These sides are ½″ longer and will overlap the short sides on the ends. Place glue on the ends of the short sides to hold the corner joints tight and along the edge of bottom, then nail both long sides into place.

Now you're ready to tack on the glides that serve as feet for the trivet. Locate on the underside of the bottom by measuring ¾″ in from each side. Mark these spots in each corner. The four plastic pads can be nailed directly into the trivet's bottom.

Turn the trivet over and check to see whether the tack glide nails are sticking through the bottom. If they are, hammer them flat, because these points will make the tile lie crooked.

Just about any type of adhesive caulk, construction adhesive, or tile mastic will hold your tile in place. If you use caulk, run a liberal bead around the trivet's base about an inch from the sides, and form an **X** in the center with adhesive. Tile mastic is spread with a notched trowel; follow the manufacturer's directions to apply. Be careful when working with these adhesives; they are both sticky and will be difficult to remove from wood sides.

After the glue is applied, set the tile in place, and slide it around to spread the glue. Then center the tile, leaving an equal space on all sides. Set the trivet aside to let the glue dry.

When the glue has hardened, sand the sides smooth, and slightly round all the edges with number 120 sandpaper. Apply a wipe-on finish to protect the wood from food stains, and your trivet is ready for action.

SHOPPING LIST

Item	Quantity
¾″ × 8″ × 8″ flakeboard or plywood (cut from scrap)	1
¼″ × 1¼″ × 36″ pine lattice or maple	1
8″ × 8″ quarry tile	1
1 set tack glides (⅞″ base)	4
number 3 finishing nails	1 box
wood glue	6-ounce bottle
number 120 sandpaper	2 sheets
tile mastic or adhesive caulk	2-ounce tube

CUTTING LIST

Part	Name	Quantity	Size	Material
A	bottom	1	8″ × 8″	¾″ plywood or flakeboard
B	short side	2	1¼″ × 8″	¼″ pine lattice or maple
C	long side	2	1¼″ × 8½″	¼″ pine lattice or maple
D	tile	1	8″ × 8″	quarry tile
E	feet	4		tack glides

Measure and cut an 8″ square out of flakeboard or plywood to make the bottom piece (A).

Clamp side stock to the table, and support it to prevent splintering. Then cut two short sides (B) to 8″ and two long sides (C) to 8½″ long.

Lay out the nail locations on sides B and C by measuring 2″ from each end and making a mark ¼″ from the bottom.

Drive number 3 finishing nail through layout marks on the sides.

Run a bead of glue down the side of the bottom.

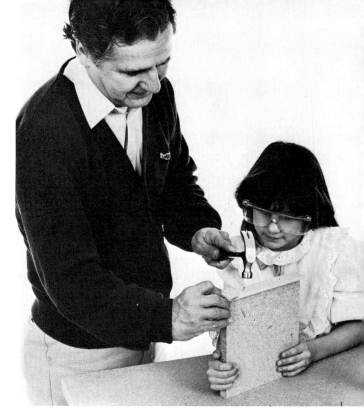

Place a short side in alignment with the end and flush with the underside of the bottom. (Repeat for other short side and two long sides.)

Locate the position of the feet by measuring ¾″ in from each side. Mark each spot on the underside of the bottom.

Drive furniture tack glides into the bottom with a hammer.

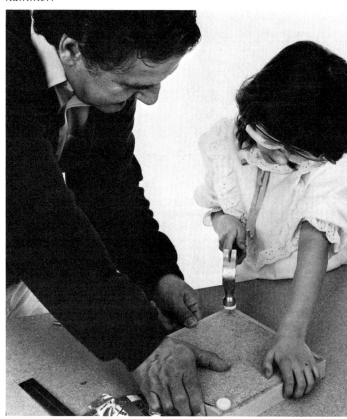

Give sides of the trivet a sanding with number 120 sandpaper. Round edges.

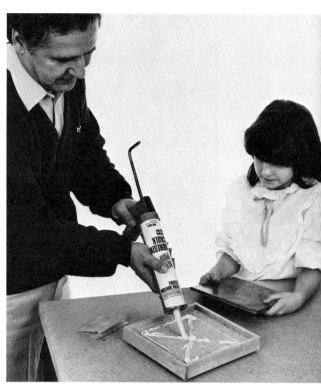

Glue tile into place with adhesive caulk or tile mastic.

Complete project with an easy-to-apply wipe-on finish.

Finished kitchen trivet.

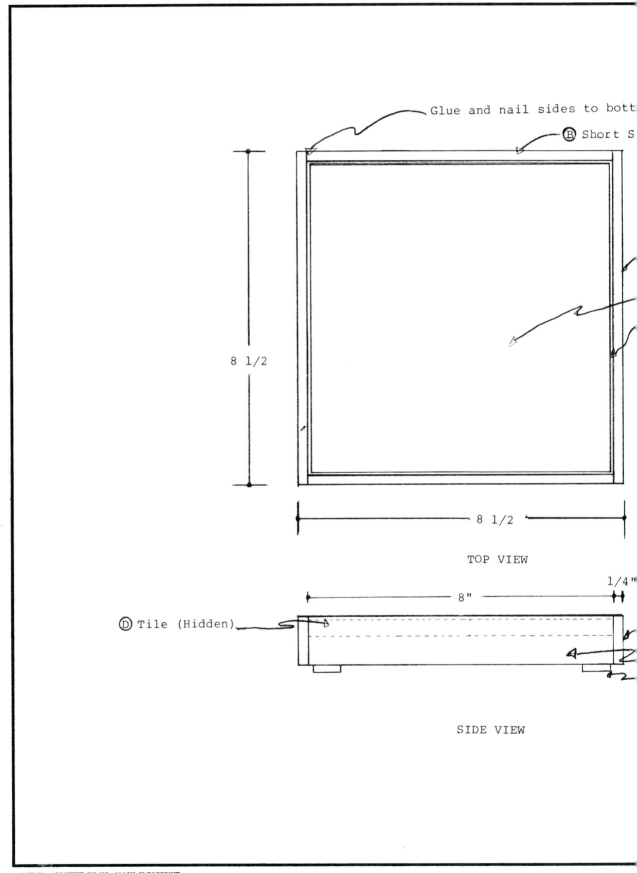

Glue and nail sides to bott

Ⓑ Short S

8 1/2

8 1/2

TOP VIEW

1/4"

8"

Ⓓ Tile (Hidden)

SIDE VIEW

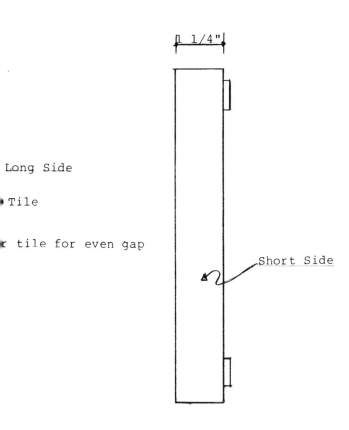

1/4"

Long Side

Tile

tile for even gap

Short Side

FRONT VIEW

Long Side

Bottom (Hidden)

Tack Glide

KITCHEN TRIVET		
	APPROVED BY:	**DRAWN BY**
DATE: 1/7/83		**REVISED**
"Build It Together"		
Katie and Gene Hamilton		**DRAWING NUMBER** 6/1

Key Rack

TIME REQUIRED: almost instant (two to three hours; time needed for cutting, building, and assembling project; does not include drying time of glue or finish)

Here's a good last-minute gift project. This key rack is easy to build, inexpensive, and just right for almost anyone. We chose a scrap piece of mahogany with pine letters for the wood contrast. Small brass cup hooks are used to hold the keys.

One stop at your home center or hardware store, and you'll be able to purchase all the materials. Most lumberyards have scrap pieces of hardwood available.

Begin building the key rack by cutting the board (A) to size. Our key rack measures 5″ × 12″, but there is no reason you can't make a larger one.

Mark the location of your key hooks with a ruler and pencil. These hooks are located ¾″ from the bottom of the board and spaced 2″ apart. Drill a ⅛″ pilot hole through the layout marks.

Drill two more ⅛″ holes in the top edge of the board 1″ from the ends for the chain screws. Then sand the board and letters with number 120 sandpaper.

Have one team member apply a small amount of glue to the back of the letters while the other spaces them evenly along the top of the board. Wipe up any excess glue with a rag.

When the glue has set, give your key rack a coat of polyurethane varnish and let it dry. Then attach the chain with two number 4 × ¾″-long brass pan-head screws. Screw in the cup hooks, and your key rack is ready to report for duty.

SHOPPING LIST

Item	Quantity
5″ × 12″ name board	1
2¾″ letters	4
brass cup hooks	5
light brass chain	12″
number 4 × ¾″ pan-head screw	2
wood glue	6-ounce bottle
number 120 sandpaper	2 sheets
finish	½ pint

CUTTING LIST

Part	Name	Quantity	Size	Material
A	board	1	½″ × 5″ × 12″	hardwood scrap

Lay out the five cup hooks ¾″ from the bottom of your board at 2″ intervals.

Drill ⅛″ pilot holes through your layout marks.

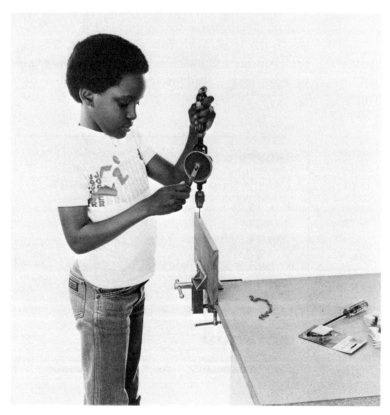

Drill two ⅛″ pilot holes in the top edge of the board 1″ from the end for the chain screws.

Sand the letters and board with number 120 sandpaper. Round the sharp corners slightly.

Attach the brass chain to the top of your key rack with two number 4 × ¾"-long screws.

Use only a small amount of glue when applying the letters.

Finished key rack.

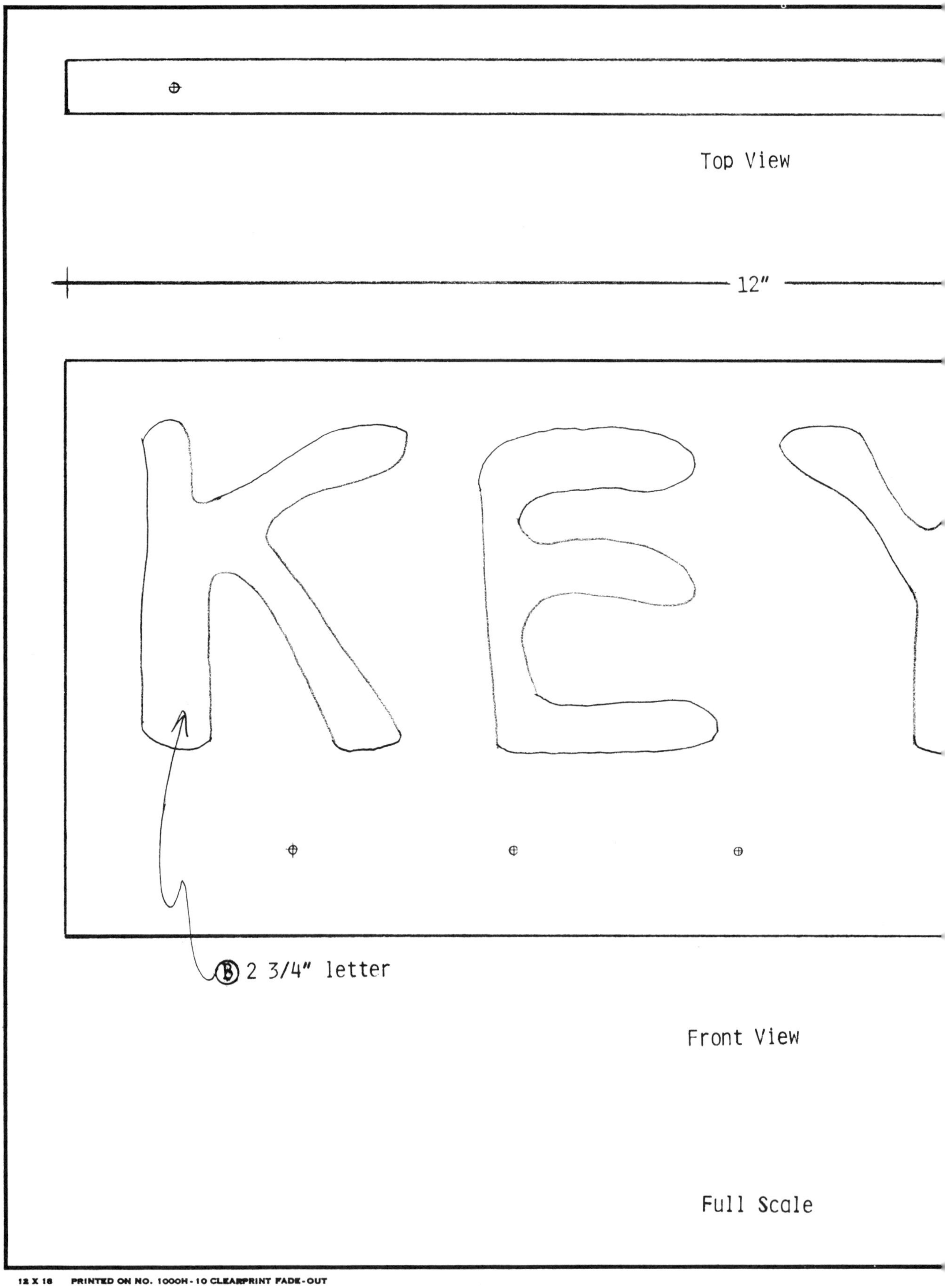

Top View

12"

KEY

B 2 3/4" letter

Front View

Full Scale

12 X 16   PRINTED ON NO. 1000H-10 CLEARPRINT FADE-OUT

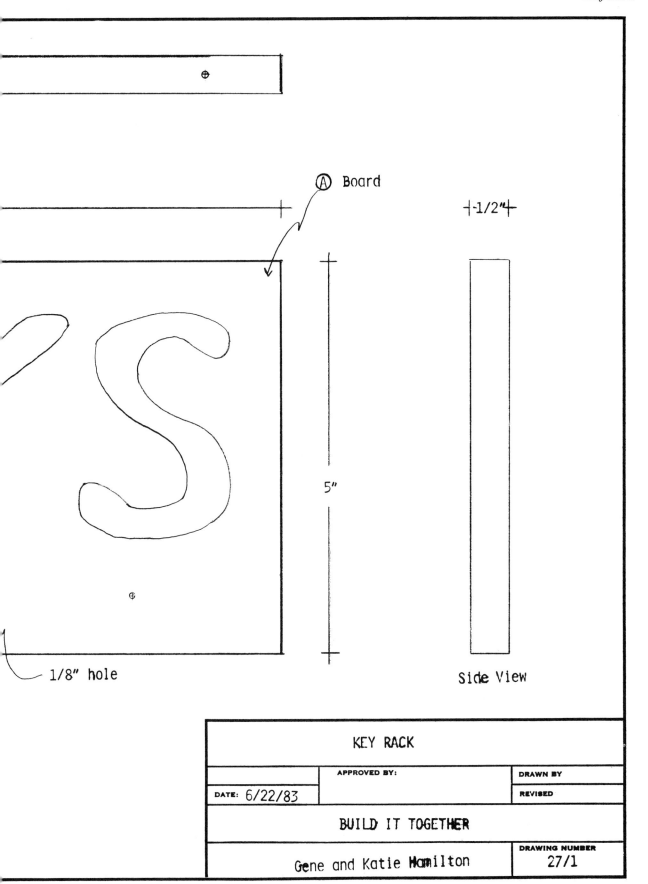

(A) Board

1/2"

5"

1/8" hole

Side View

		KEY RACK		
	APPROVED BY:		DRAWN BY	
DATE: 6/22/83			REVISED	
		BUILD IT TOGETHER		
	Gene and Katie Hamilton		DRAWING NUMBER 27/1	

Toy Crate

TIME REQUIRED: half day (time needed for cutting, building, and assembling project; does not include drying time of glue or finish)

Although it looks like a shipping crate, our easy-to-cut-and-assemble toy crate is made to keep a kid's stuff all in one place. Whether it stores sporting gear, a doll and all its accessories, or just toys, our crate solves the "keeping-it-all-together" problem.

We used slats made of pine lattice for sides and 2″ × 2″ pine to reinforce corners. To make it look authentic, Mike's crate is stenciled with his name.

Begin building your crate by measuring the long slats (A), following dimensions on the Cutting List. With thirteen pieces to cut, both partners can take turns sawing. The short slats (B) are cut next; notice that these pieces are ½″ shorter than the A pieces. The corner posts (C) are cut from 2″ × 2″ stock, as are the bottom rails (D).

After all cutting is finished, begin assembly by gluing and nailing with number 4 box nails a short slat to one of the bottom rails. Make sure the

pieces are aligned at both ends and along the bottom.

Place the corner posts (C) in position so they butt on top of the bottom rail and are aligned with its end. Place a little glue where the slat meets the corner posts, and then nail them together.

Glue and nail a slat to the top of one of the corner posts. Align it, and before you drive in a second nail, check that the end is square. Then glue and nail the center two slats.

Assemble the other end in the same manner. Next, place the two end sections on their sides opposite one another. Apply glue to the end of a long slat, and nail it in place flush with the bottom and square with the end. Do the same at the other end. Glue and nail on the top slat next, and check the crate for squareness. Put in the center two slats, then turn the crate over, and glue and nail on the other side.

The bottom slats go on next. Turn your crate over so that the bottom rails are exposed. All the bottom slats are nailed to the bottom rail. Put in the outside slats first. Evenly space the remaining slats, then glue and nail in position.

Your crate is ready to finish. An easy-to-apply

finish of spray varnish or sealer will protect the wood. The final touch is personalizing the crate with the builder's name.

Make a stencil by tracing inexpensive block letters, available at any stationery store, on to lightweight cardboard. The older team member should act as surgeon when carefully cutting out the letters because razor knives are sharp.

Place paper around the stencil to protect the crate from overspray. Decide how you want your letters spaced, and then tape the stencil in place. Use spray paint, and shoot it through the stencil to create your name.

SHOPPING LIST

Item	Quantity
¼″ × 3½″ × 10′ pine lattice	4
1½″ × 1½″ × 10′ (2″ × 2″) pine furring	1
carpenter's glue	8-ounce bottle
number 4 box nails	1 pound
number 120 sandpaper	2 sheets
⅜″ rope	3′
polyurethane varnish	1 quart

CUTTING LIST

Part	Name	Quantity	Size	Material
A	long slat	13	¼″ × 3½″ × 20″	pine lattice
B	short slat	8	¼″ × 3½″ × 19½″	pine lattice
C	corner post	4	1½″ × 1½″ × 14¾″	2″ × 2″ pine
D	rail	2	1½″ × 1½″ × 19½″	2″ × 2″ pine

Lay out the length of slats A and B with a tape and combination square to assure a straight cut.

Secure the slats to the table, and cut them to size.

Apply glue to the first bottom rail (D).

Place a short slat on the bottom rail along the ends, and check that it is flush with the bottom edge. Nail in place.

Glue and nail a slat (B) to the top of the corner posts, and check the crate for squareness.

To assemble the two ends, place a long slat even with bottom edge and flush with the ends, and glue and nail it into place.

The first slat of the bottom is glued and nailed to the bottom rail.

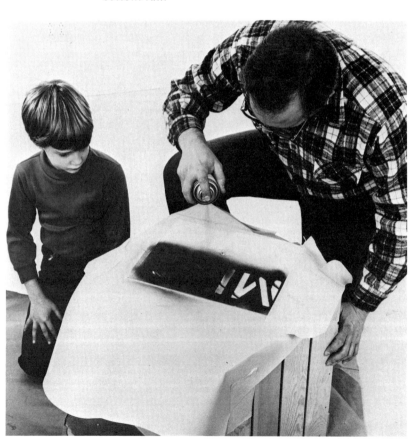

Hold the spray can about a foot from the crate, and paint the letters.

Finished toy crate.

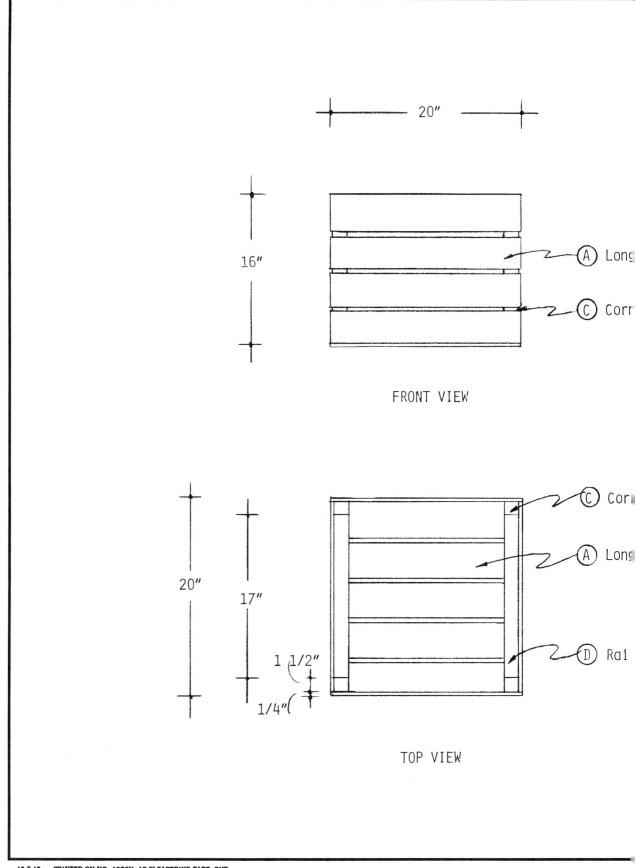

20″

16″

(A) Long

(C) Cor

FRONT VIEW

20″

17″

1 1/2″

1/4″

(C) Cor

(A) Long

(D) Rai

TOP VIEW

12 X 18   PRINTED ON NO. 1000H - 10 CLEARPRINT FADE-OUT

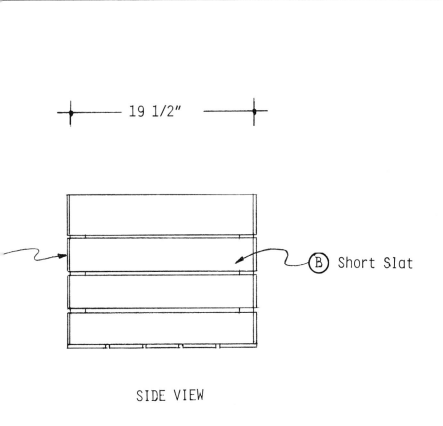

19 1/2"

B Short Slat

SIDE VIEW

Toy Crate		
APPROVED BY:		DRAWN BY
DATE: 1/20/83		REVISED
BUILD IT TOGETHER		
Gene and Katie Hamilton		DRAWING NUMBER 8/1

Poster Clock

TIME REQUIRED: one day (time needed for cutting, building, and assembling project; does not include drying time of glue or finish)

E.T. has a ticker! We gave our favorite alien a time-piece—a quartz movement clock, that is. This poster-clock project requires almost a whole day to create, but the result is well worth it.

We had our poster mounted onto a heavy board at a picture-framing store, which cost under $10. Purchasing the wallpaper sizing, cellulose paste, and heavy board cost about the same. If you have those supplies on hand, you might want to mount the poster yourself.

With our poster on the board, we used 1¾"-wide lattice and parting stop to construct a deep frame to house an inexpensive quartz clock movement, E.T.'s ticker. The tiny hour dots are paper stick-ons that can be found at a stationery store.

The frame is constructed first. Begin by laying out the sides (A) and top and bottom pieces (B) on the pine lattice. Then lay out the side and top and bottom stops (C and D) on parting stop. See the Cutting List for all lengths. An inexpensive miter box will guide the apprentice when cutting these parts to length. Square ends are important for good-looking corner joints.

Parts C and D are glued to the side and top and bottom pieces (A and B). Drive small finishing nails into the ½" sides of C and D, and then apply glue to the edge of C. Place a scrap of parting stop with its ¾" side flat on top of A and aligned with its end. This piece acts as a spacer to position part C ¾" from the end of A. One team member should hold the spacer in place while the other nails C in place. Assemble the other side of the frame in the same manner.

The top and bottom parts are glued to D using a piece of ¼" lattice as a spacer. Place the lattice on edge, even with the end of B. Glue and nail parting stop D in place ¼" from the end and even with the front of B.

The sides, top, and bottom are glued together next. Coat all mating surfaces of the corners with glue. Nail the frame together with small finishing nails driven through side A into the end of D. Place a nail as far from the edge of A as possible to prevent its end from splitting.

55

String about a dozen rubber bands (depending on size) together to form a temporary clamp. Place the frame face down on a flat surface and loop the rubber bands around it. Pull the ends tight and loop them over scrap wood, then twist the piece to hold the rubber bands together. Set the frame aside until the glue is dry.

We chose to place our clock in the light area around E.T.'s heart. This space measures about 6½" in diameter. If you choose a different poster, vary the diameter of your clock face to suit your design.

Use a compass to lay out the clock-face template. It's easy to mark the hour positions on the circle if you first divide the circle into quarters, just as if you're cutting a pie. Next, put the compass point at the 3 o'clock position and set it to the radius of the circle. Swing it until the pencil intersects the circle arc, and mark this point. Then swing your compass in the opposite direction, and mark the other intersection. These points are the 1 o'clock and 5 o'clock points. Do this from the 6, 9, and 12 o'clock positions, and all hour positions will be accurately marked on the circle arc.

Cut out your clock template and place it on the poster. Mark the center of the clock face on your poster by pushing the compass point through the small hole in the center of the paper template. Remove it, and drill a ⅜" hole through cardboard for the clockworks' shaft.

Replace the template, and use it as a guide when placing the self-adhesive dots or numbers on the poster face.

Screw the clockworks' shaft through the hole, and then thread on the locking nut. The hour hand slips on the shaft, and the minute hand fits over the smaller keyed shaft in the center. Turn the time by adjusting the knob on the back of the clockworks until the minute hand points directly at the 12. Then adjust the hour hand (it has a press fit and will move around the clock shaft) to point to any hour.

An acorn dress nut is supplied by the manufacturer. Thread it on carefully, and do not overtighten.

All that is left to do to get E.T.'s heart ticking is to place an AA-size battery in the clockworks and turn on the switch.

Attach your poster clock to a wall with plastic wall anchors. We used large picture-hanging brackets and finishing nails driven into the lath of a plaster wall. If your walls are covered with drywall, use plastic wall anchors. Tighten the anchor screws until their heads are ⅛" from the wall surface, then hook the picture brackets over the screw heads.

SHOPPING LIST

Item	Quantity
¼" × 1¾" × 12' pine lattice	1
½" × ¾" × 12' parting stop	1
24" × 36" mounted poster	1
wood glue	6-ounce tube
number 120 sandpaper	2 sheets
finish	1 pint
quartz clock movement	1 (short shaft)
clock hands	2
Avery stick-on dots	1 package
large picture hanging bracket	2

CUTTING LIST

Part	Name	Quantity	Size	Material
A	side	2	¼" × 1¾" × 35"	pine lattice
B	top/bottom	2	¼" × 1¾" × 23½"	pine lattice
C	side stop	2	½" × ¾" × 33½"	pine parting stop
D	top/bottom	2	½" × ¾" × 23"	pine parting stop

Lay out all the pieces to the lengths specified on the Cutting List.

Cut the frame parts A, B, C, and D with a miter box to assure square ends.

Predrive small finishing nails into the ½" side of parts C and D.

Apply glue to the back of parts C and D.

Place a scrap of parting stop flush with the end of A to help position C, then nail it into place.

Place a scrap of lattice flush with the end of B to help position D, then nail it into place.

Put glue on the ends of the frame assembly, and drive a nail through A into the end of D.

Use rubber bands to hold the frame together while the glue dries.

Use a compass to draw the clock face. Set compass to radius, and mark the locations of the numbers or dots.

Place the mounted poster on a flat surface with scrap behind, and drill a ⅝" hole where you want the clock center.

Center the dial template over the clock and lay on dots or numbers.

Install clock hands according to the manufacturer's directions.

Finished poster clock.

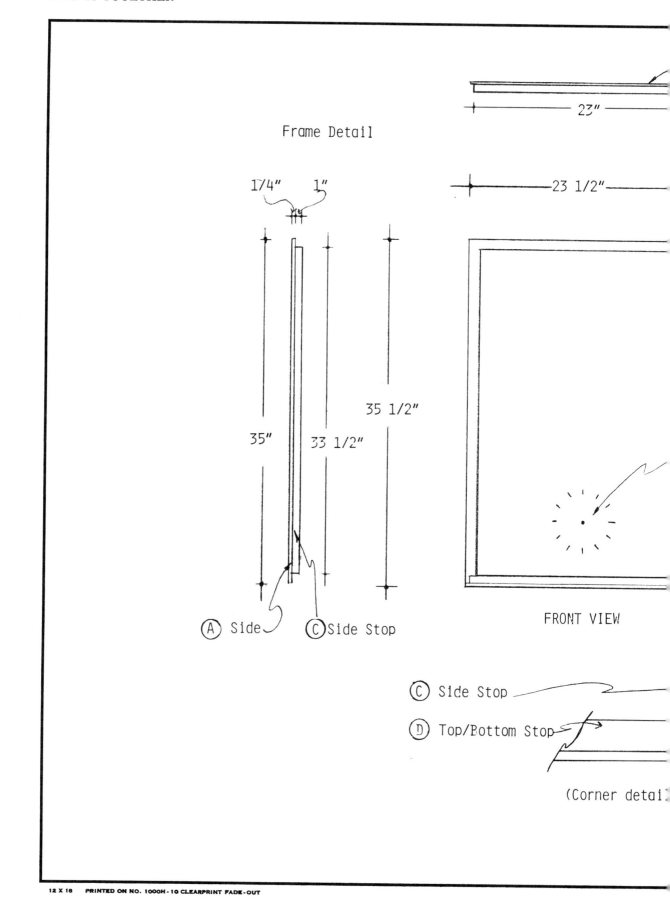

Frame Detail

1/4"   1"

35 1/2"

35"   33 1/2"

Ⓐ Side   Ⓒ Side Stop

23"

23 1/2"

FRONT VIEW

Ⓒ Side Stop

Ⓓ Top/Bottom Stop

(Corner detail)

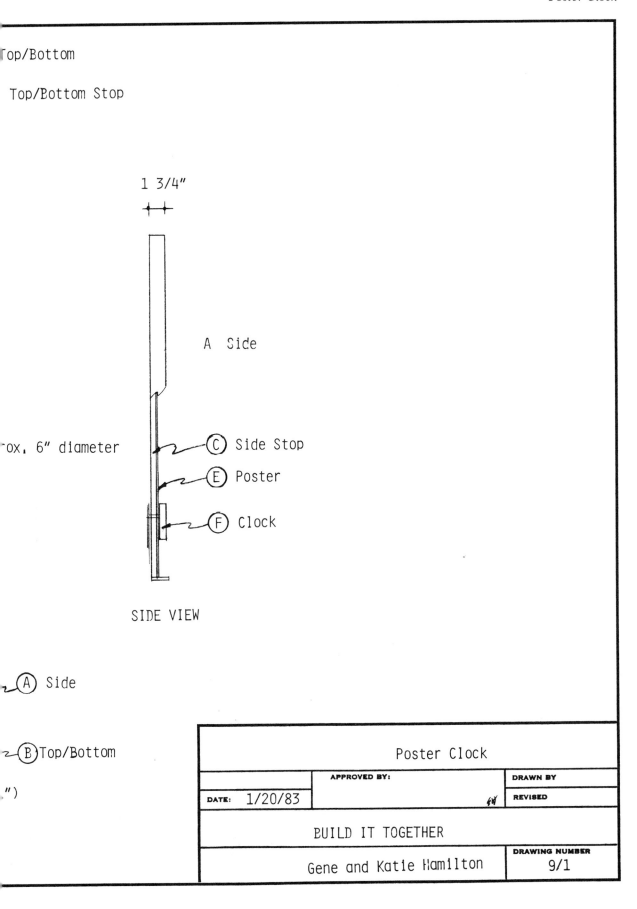

Top/Bottom

Top/Bottom Stop

1 3/4"

A Side

rox, 6" diameter

C Side Stop

E Poster

F Clock

SIDE VIEW

A Side

B Top/Bottom

")

Poster Clock		
APPROVED BY:		DRAWN BY
DATE: 1/20/83		REVISED
BUILD IT TOGETHER		
Gene and Katie Hamilton		DRAWING NUMBER 9/1

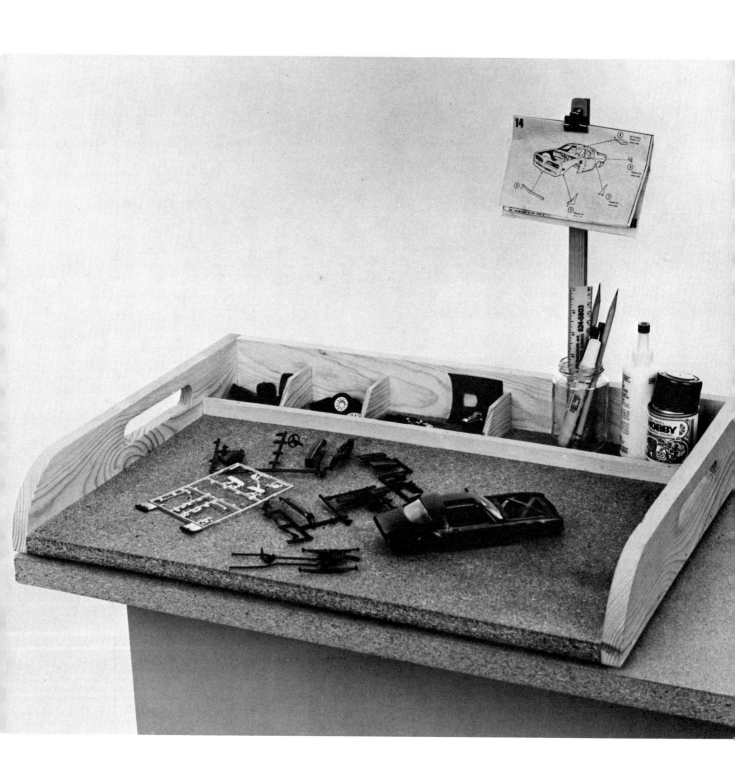

Model Building Board

TIME REQUIRED: half day (time needed for cutting, building, and assembling project; does not include drying time of glue or finish)

Here's our solution to a problem all model builders face—where to work and how to keep all the parts neat and organized. This model building board can be placed on top of a desk, kitchen table, or any well-lighted surface.

It's portable, with handles for easy carrying. The sturdy base rests on mar-proof feet that protect your furniture from a young modeler's glue or paint. Along the back of the board are four compartments, handy for organizing parts and supplies, and an instruction holder with a metal clip, available at most stationery stores.

This board is easy to construct and has a tough particle board base. We found ¾"-thick 18"-wide shelving at our home center and based the design around it. Purchase 2' of this material for a ready-made base. If your lumberyard does not stock shelving that wide, have them cut the base from a quarter sheet.

Since the back and sides (B and C) are made from 1" × 4" pine stock, only their length need be measured (see Cutting List). Lay this out, and then cut the sides and back.

Both sides have a 3½"-radius rounded end. Use a compass to scribe the arc. Clamp the side to the table, and use a coping saw to cut the rounded corner.

The handle slots are laid out by marking the location of the slot end holes. Measure 5½" from the square end and 1¼" from the top edge, and make your first mark. The other hole is located 8½" from the rounded end and 1¼" from the top. Secure your side to the table, and drill a 1" hole through these locater marks.

Connect the two outside edges of these end holes with straight lines. Then use a keyhole or coping saw to cut from hole to hole, creating the handle slot.

Give the back and sides a sanding to remove any rough corners. Wrap sandpaper around a short piece of scrap when sanding the inside of the handle slots.

Your board is ready for assembly. Predrive number 3 finishing nails 3" apart through the sides and back about ½″ from the bottom. Run a bead of glue along the back edge of the bottom. Place the back piece in position, lining it up flush and even with the ends of the bottom. Have one team member hold the bottom in position while the other drives in the nails.

The sides are glued and nailed in place the same way. Put glue on the sides of the bottom piece and the ends of the back. Align the sides with the front edge of the bottom and nail them into place. Then drive three evenly spaced nails into the back edge of the sides to hold them tight against the back of the board.

Set the board aside to allow the glue to dry while you cut the compartments. The compartment front (D) is cut from ½″ × ¾″ parting stop, and the dividers from ¼″ × 1¾″ lattice. Following lengths on the Cutting List, cut the front, and cut out the full-size template for the sides (E). Trace the template for the sides on the lattice, and cut out the remaining three pieces.

Place a compartment divider temporarily in each back corner, against the sides of the model board, to hold the compartment front in place while you glue and nail it with several evenly spaced number 3 nails. Then put glue on the front and back edges of the compartment pieces, and space them to form four compartments—two 3″ wide, one 4″ wide, and one 6″ wide.

Cut a 12″ piece of parting stop for the instruction holder (F) and attach the spring clip (G) to one end with a number 6 wood screw. At the other end of the holder, drill a ³⁄₁₆″ hole 1″ from the end. Place the instruction holder in position on the back of the board and make a pencil mark through the hole on the backboard. Drill a ¹⁄₁₆″ pilot hole through this mark, and mount the instruction holder with a number 6 × 1″ wood screw. Attach one furniture foot to the bottom of each corner.

Your model building board is ready for finishing. A coat of varnish will protect the wood. Give the bottom a single coat to seal it; more finishing will lift if modeling cement is spilled on it. The flakeboard is tough and will stand up to cutting. When the surface becomes coated with globs of glue and paint, scrape it with a razor, give it a light sanding, and recoat with finish.

SHOPPING LIST

Item	Quantity
¾″ flakeboard	scrap cut off at least 24″ × 18″
1″ × 4″ × 6′ number 2 pine	1
½″ × ¾″ × 24″ parting stop	1
¼″ × 1¾″ × 12″ pine lattice	1
number 3 finishing nails	small box
wood glue	6-ounce bottle
small spring clip	1
number 6 × 1″ wood screw	2
number 120 sandpaper	2 sheets
furniture feet	4
finish	1 pint

CUTTING LIST

Part	Name	Quantity	Size	Material
A	bottom	1	¾″ × 24″ × 18″	flakeboard
B	back	1	¾″ × 24″ × 3½″	pine 1 × 4
C	side	2	¾″ × 18½″ × 3½″	pine 1 × 4
D	compartment front	1	½″ × 24″ × ¾″	pine parting stop
E	compartment side	3	¼″ × 3″ × 1¾″	pine lattice
F	instruction holder	1	½″ × ¾″ × 12″	pine parting stop

Use a tape measure to lay out the lengths of the back and sides (B and C). All are cut from 1″ × 4″ stock.

Secure the wood to the table and cut parts to length.

Lay out the 3½″ corner radius on the side ends with a compass.

On each side, make a mark 5½″ from the back (square end) and 1¼″ from the top edge to locate the position of the pilot hole for the handle slot. The other pilot hole is located 8½″ from the front (rounded end).

Drill a 1″ pilot hole to form the ends of the handle cutouts.

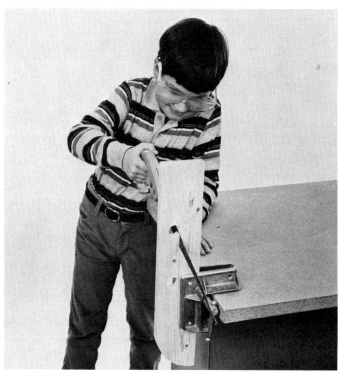

Use a keyhole or coping saw, and cut from pilot hole to pilot hole to form the handle slot.

Sand the sides and back, and then predrive number 3 finishing nails through the outside face ½″ from the bottom.

Put glue along the back edge of the bottom.

Trace the template for the compartment sides on the lattice, and cut out the three remaining pieces.

Place a compartment side at both back corners of the model board to align the compartment front while nailing. Install the compartment front with glue and nails.

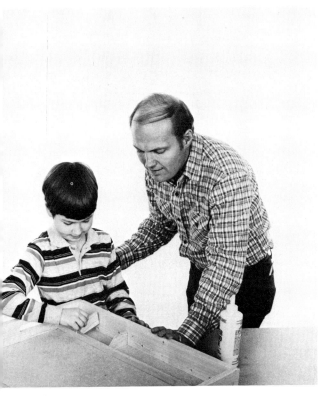

Put glue on the back and front edges of the compartment sides, and place them to form two 3", one 4", and one 6" compartment.

Finished model building board.

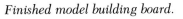

25 1/2"

(E) Compartment Side

3" 4" 6" 3"

(B) Bac

(C) Sid

(D) Compartment Front

(A) Bott

24"

TOP VIEW

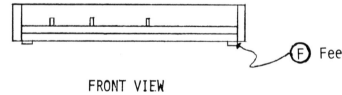

(F) Fee

FRONT VIEW

12 X 18   PRINTED ON NO. 1000H-10 CLEARPRINT FADE-OUT

3 1/2"

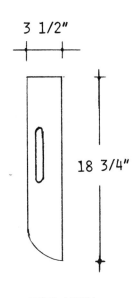

18 3/4"

SIDE VIEW

1"

1"

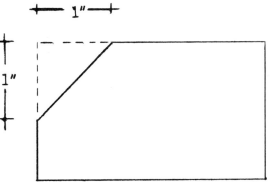

Compartment Side
FULL SIZE

Model Building Board		
	APPROVED BY:	DRAWN BY
DATE: 1/19/83		REVISED
BUILD IT TOGETHER		
Gene and Katie Hamilton		DRAWING NUMBER 10/1

Bulletin Board

TIME REQUIRED: half day (time needed for cutting, building, and assembling project; does not include drying time of glue or finish)

Who couldn't use this handsome bulletin board? Whether it's a gift for someone's office, kitchen, or bedroom or for the builder's own room, this customized bulletin board will be put to constant use.

The board is simple to construct. We used cardboard, precut cork panels, and corner molding for the frame. You can personalize the board with inexpensive wood letters available at all home centers.

The backing board (C) is cut from a quarter sheet of ⅛″ hardboard. Most lumberyards will cut the quarter sheet in half for a small charge.

Cardboard is glued to the backing to provide a soft surface for the stickpin points. Regular corrugated cardboard will do. Run a ¼″ bead of construction adhesive along the perimeter of the backing, and then fill in the remaining area with an **S** pattern.

Place the cardboard on the backing, and press firmly to spread adhesive. Then turn the sandwich over, and trim the cardboard flush with the backing board.

With the cardboard facing up, apply more adhesive to the board in the same pattern. Then place cork panels in position. Turn the unit over, and put some heavy objects on the backing while the adhesive sets.

The sides (A) and top and bottom (B) are cut next. The measurements on the Cutting List are from one point of the 45-degree miter cut to the other. When measuring, make a 45-degree cut on one end, and then measure from this pointed end.

Mark the lengths for the sides, top, and bottom on the molding piece, and then put it into the miter box so that the mark is aligned with the miter slot in the box. Make your cut so that the 45-degree point comes out at the mark.

Parts A and B are glued to the board with construction adhesive. Run a bead of adhesive down the **V** of the molding. Be careful not to get adhesive on the lip that will touch the cork; any adhesive on the lip will squeeze out on the cork front of your bulletin board. Put wood glue on the miter joints, and place the sides, top, and bottom in position.

Tie several rubber bands together to make a

temporary clamp. Place the bulletin board face down on a flat surface, and press the frame firmly in place. Stretch the rubber bands around the frame, and loop their ends over a piece of scrap wood. Double-check the alignment of the frame, and set it aside to dry.

To put on the brackets, glue a piece of scrap to the backboard along the top of the bulletin board. Screw heavy-duty picture-hanging brackets to the scrap with number 6 × ¾" screws.

David personalized his bulletin board by gluing on wood letters. Apply the same finish you're using for the frame to the fronts of the letters before you glue them in place. When the finish has dried, put a small amount of adhesive on the back of the letters and align them. A short name can be run across the top, while smaller letters will spell out a longer name that runs along the side of the board.

After the glue has dried, sand the frame with number 120 paper. We used a wipe-on finish to seal the frame, but you can also paint your bulletin board. Be careful when applying finish around the cork. To keep the finish from getting on the cork, place a piece of cardboard tight against the frame to shield the face.

SHOPPING LIST

Item	Quantity
¾" pine outside corner molding	12'
⅛" hardboard	¼ sheet
corrugated cardboard	several pieces to cover 24" × 36" area
sheet cork	24" × 36"
construction adhesive	1 tube
4" precut letters	as needed
wood glue	6-ounce bottle
picture-hanging bracket	2
finish or paint	1 pint
number 120 sandpaper	2 sheets

CUTTING LIST

Part	Name	Quantity	Size	Material
A	side (frame)	2	¾" × ¾" × 36½"	pine outside corner molding
B	top/bottom (frame)	2	¾" × ¾" × 24½"	pine outside corner molding
C	backing	1	⅛" × 24" × 36"	hardboard
D	cardboard facing	1	¼" × 24" × 36"	corrugated cardboard
E	cork	1	⅛" × 24" × 36"	sheet cork

Run a ¼″ bead of construction adhesive along the perimeter of the backing (C). Then run S beads in the center.

Use a razor knife to trim the cardboard flush with the backing. Masking tape shown here is not necessary.

Apply adhesive to the cardboard side of the board, and then place the cork sheets on it.

Use an inexpensive miter box to make the 45-degree corner cuts.

Measure the length of the sides, top, and bottom. The dimensions in the Cutting List are from one point of the miter cut to the other.

Apply adhesive to the inside of the sides, top, and bottom. To prevent adhesive from squeezing out on the face of the cork, be careful not to get any adhesive on the lip that touches the cork.

Tie rubber bands together to form a temporary clamp. Wrap it around the frame, and secure the rubber bands by wrapping them around a piece of scrap wood.

Glue a piece of scrap to the top of the backing board. Then attach two picture-hanging brackets with number 6 × ¾" screws.

Finished bulletin board.

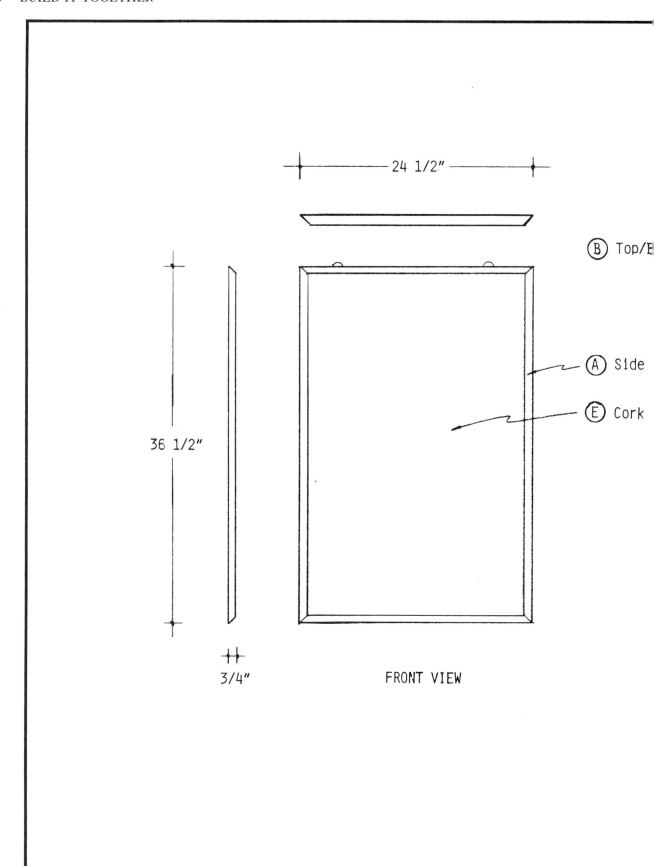

24 1/2"

(B) Top/E

(A) Side

(E) Cork

36 1/2"

3/4"

FRONT VIEW

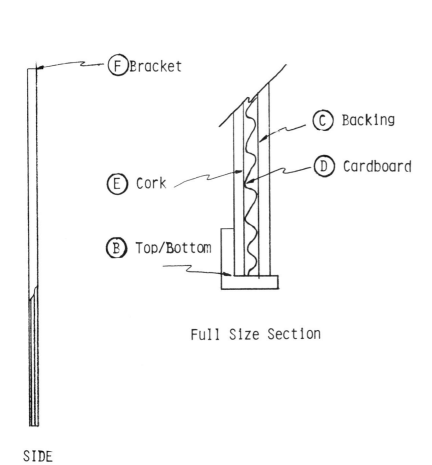

(F) Bracket

(C) Backing

(D) Cardboard

(E) Cork

(B) Top/Bottom

Full Size Section

SIDE

	APPROVED BY:		DRAWN BY
DATE: 1/20/83		*4f*	REVISED
BUILD IT TOGETHER			
Gene and Katie Hamilton		DRAWING NUMBER	11/1

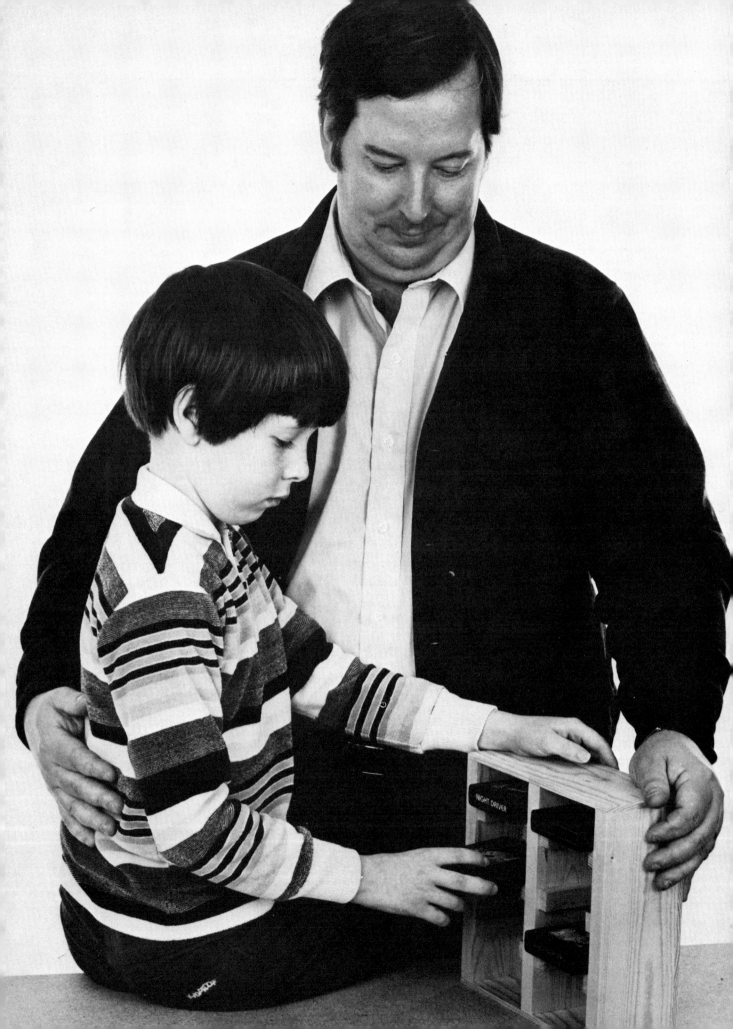

Electronic Game Cartridge Holder

TIME REQUIRED: half day (time needed for cutting, building, and assembling project; does not include drying time of glue or finish)

Does your television do double duty as an arcade game? Keeping electronic game cartridges safe and organized can become a problem as their number multiplies. Here is an easy-to-make modular game cartridge holder that will keep everything shipshape.

Our cartridge cube holds eight games and is made of pine, finished naturally. Several may be constructed and stacked together to fit your expanding game library.

Construction is easy, although there are many small parts to cut. Use a miter box to ensure square ends. Following the lengths on the Cutting List, cut the three partitions (A), the top and bottom (B), and three back parts (C and D) to size, but do not cut D to width now.

The supports (E) are cut from parting stop. Since a dozen are needed, we made a gauge by clamping a piece of scrap to the table. Adjust the

position of the miter box so that the distance from the cutoff slot and the stop gauge is 3¼". Then all you have to do is push the parting stop through the miter box until it hits the stop block, and cut. Repeat, and all the supports will be the same length without your having to measure each one individually. Take turns cutting. While one cuts, the other can sand the support pieces smooth with number 120 sandpaper.

Use a square to mark the location of the supports on the sides of two partitions, drawing layout lines 1½", 2¼", and 2¼" from the bottom of the partitions. Draw layout lines on both sides of the center partition.

The supports are glued and nailed into place using ⅛" × 18 wire brads. The bottom edges of the supports are aligned on the layout lines. The supports should be flush with the back edge of the partition pieces, setting them back ¼" from the front edge of the partitions. Before you assemble the second side, check that you have a right and left side, and make any necessary correction. Do not put in center partition now.

The top and bottom are put on next. Glue and nail the partitions flush with the ends of the top and bottom, and then place center partition in position. After installing the center partition, turn the cube face down (the front is the side with the setback supports), and nail and glue on the two larger back parts (C), starting at the bottom of the cube. Place the small back part (D) in position, and mark its width by running a pencil line along the top of the cube. Now cut D to width, and nail and glue it into place.

Sand your cube with number 120 sandpaper. If the ends or back extends slightly beyond the sides, place a piece of sandpaper on a flat surface, and run the cube over the paper. Your cube sides will then be smooth and square.

We finished our cube with a transparent wipe-on sealer. You might want to paint yours a bright color, especially if you're going to make several.

SHOPPING LIST

Item	Quantity
1″ × 4″ pine	4′
¼″ × 3½″ pine lattice	6′
½″ × ¾″ pine parting stop	5′
⅞″ × 18 wire brads	small box
wood glue	6-ounce bottle
number 120 sandpaper	2 sheets
finish or paint	1 pint

CUTTING LIST

Part	Name	Quantity	Size	Material
A	partitions	3	¾″ × 3½″ × 8½″	1″ × 4″ pine
B	top/bottom	2	¼″ × 3½″ × 9¼″	pine lattice
C	back	2	¼″ × 3½″ × 9¼″	pine lattice
D	small back	1	¼″ × 1½″ × 9¼″	pine lattice
E	supports	12	½″ × ¾″ × 3¼″	pine parting stop

To make cutting the supports (E) easy, clamp a scrap block to your table 3¼″ from the cutting slot of the miter box to form a stop. After each cut, slide the wood to the stop.

Glue and nail the supports to the inside faces of the side partitions with ⅞″ × 18 wire brads. Do not put in the center partition.

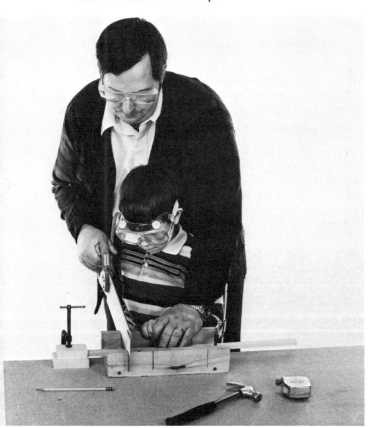

Glue and nail the top to the side partitions. Keep the top ends flush with the sides of the partitions, making sure the top aligns with the front of the partitions.

Glue and nail on two larger back parts (C). Keep panels aligned with sides.

Install the center partition 4⅝" from either side of the cube. Use glue and ⅞" × 18 wire brads to put into place.

Place small back part (D) in place, and mark its width. Remove, and cut it to size, then glue and nail it into place.

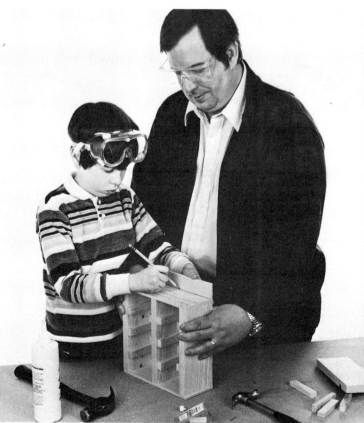

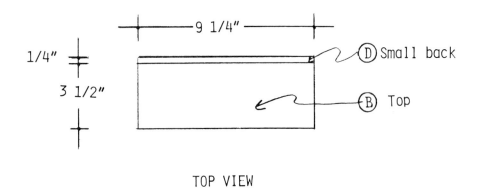

1/4"

3 1/2"

9 1/4"

(D) Small back

(B) Top

TOP VIEW

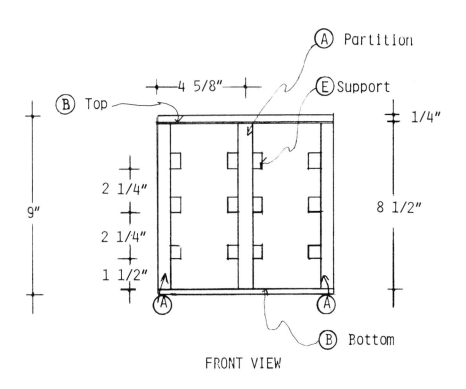

(A) Partition

(E) Support

(B) Top

4 5/8"

1/4"

9"

2 1/4"

2 1/4"

1 1/2"

8 1/2"

(A)   (A)

(B) Bottom

FRONT VIEW

12 X 18   PRINTED ON NO. 1000H-10 CLEARPRINT FADE-OUT

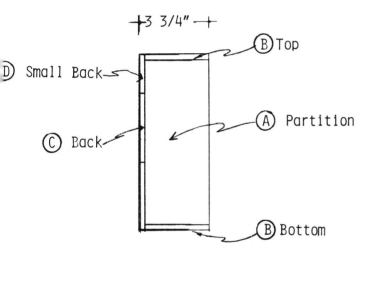

SIDE VIEW

	Game Cartridge Holder		
	APPROVED BY:		DRAWN BY
DATE: 2/5/83			REVISED
	Gene and Katie Hamilton		
BUILD IT TOGETHER			DRAWING NUMBER 12/1

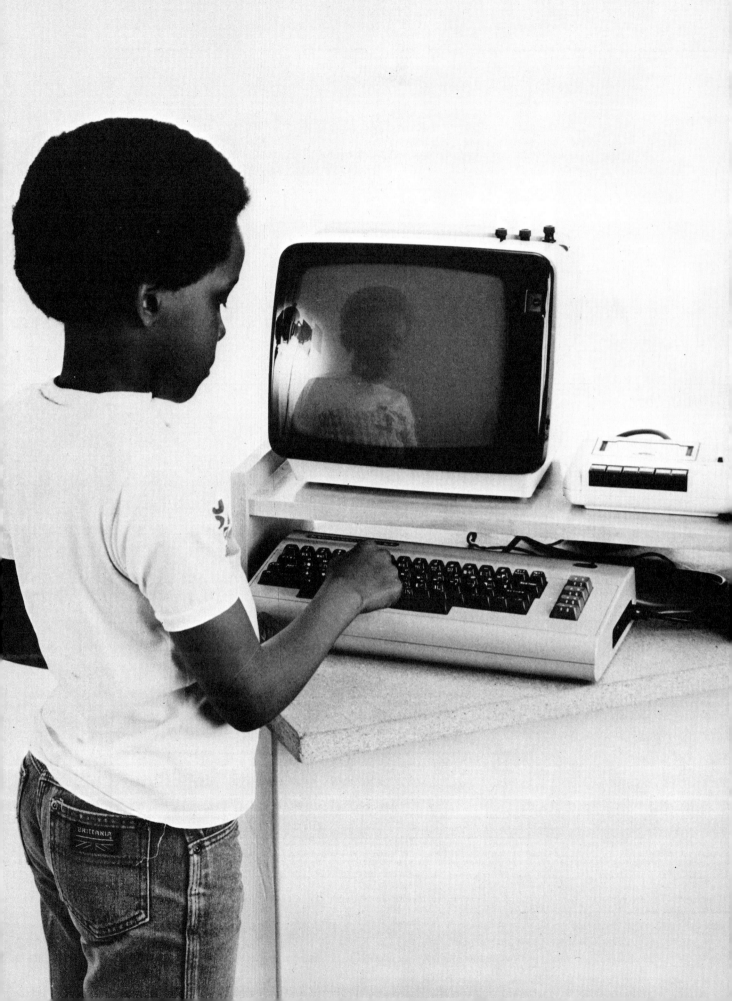

Home Computer Station

TIME REQUIRED: half day (time needed for cutting, building, and assembling project; does not include drying time of glue or finish)

Welcome to the computer age! If there's a computer in your house, the junior programmer has probably commandeered it to his room. With its maze of wires and component parts, a home computer often becomes a tangled mess. Here is a quick-to-make solution to this problem.

Our computer work station is designed for the Commodore 64 and is wide enough for the tape drive (for data and program storage) to sit conveniently beside it. But the station is so easy to build, you can modify the dimensions to fit just about any home computer.

You can make your computer station from a single 6'-piece of 1″ × 12″ lumber. Cut the sides (A) and shelf (B) from 1″ × 12″ stock, following lengths on the Cutting List. Then cut the support (C) to length and to width. Clamp a straight piece of wood on the support to guide your saw.

The bottom edge of the shelf is located 4″ from the bottom of the sides. Use a combination square to draw a straight line across the sides to act as a guide when assembling your station.

On the other side of the sides, which will face out, draw another layout line 1⅝″ down from the top. Then drive four equally spaced number 6 finishing nails along this layout line. Place the outside nails 2″ from the ends of the sides. Then run a bead of glue down the edge of the shelf, and have one team member hold it upright while the other nails on the sides. Note that the shelf is set back ¼″ from the front edge of the sides. Turn your station over, and glue and nail on the other end.

Put glue on the ends and top edge of the support, then place it into position along the underside of the bottom flush with its back edge. Nail it in place with number 6 finishing nails driven through the sides and along the back edge of the shelf.

Sand all edges smooth with number 120 sandpaper. Also sand any glue marks that might have seeped out of the joints.

We finished our station with a coat of quick-drying white shellac and rubbed it to a high gloss with 0000 steel wool and paste wax. This is an easy-to-apply finish that resists finger marks.

SHOPPING LIST

Item	Quantity
1″ × 12″ pine	6′
number 6 finishing nails	1 dozen
wood glue	6-ounce bottle
number 120 sandpaper	2 sheets
finish	1 pint
0000 steel wool	1 package

CUTTING LIST

Part	Name	Quantity	Size	Material
A	side	2	¾″ × 11¼″ × 6″	1″ × 12″ pine
B	shelf	1	¾″ × 10¼″ × 22″	1″ × 12″ pine
C	support	1	¾″ × 2″ × 22″	1″ × 12″ pine

On the inside face of the sides (A) mark a line 2″ from the top. On the outer side, mark a line 1⅝″ from the top.

Drive four evenly spaced nails along the line 1⅝″ from the top of the sides. Put glue on the ends of the shelf (B).

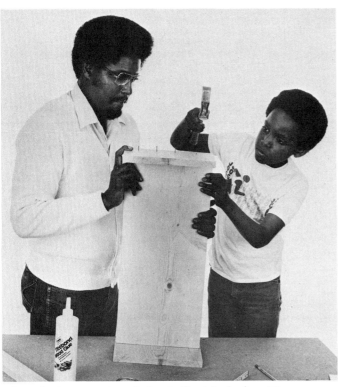

Align the bottom edge of the shelf with the line 2″ from the top of the side. Then adjust the front edge of the shelf to ¼″ back from the front edge of the side.

Now you're ready to glue and nail on the shelf. Set all nailheads below the surface of the wood with a nail set.

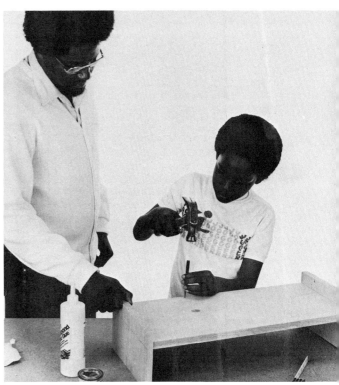

Sand your computer station smooth with number 120 paper.

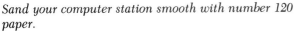

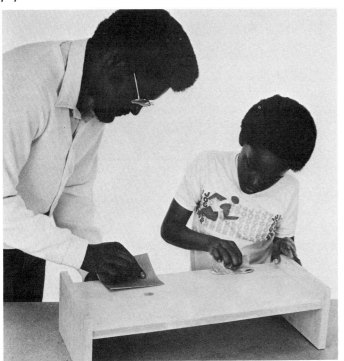

Finished home computer station.

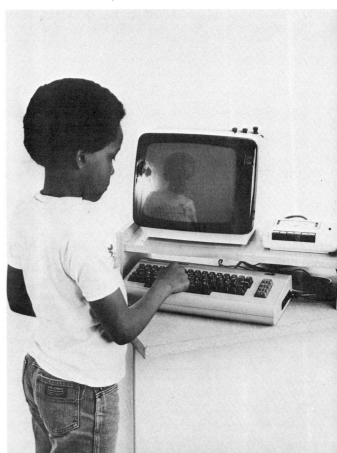

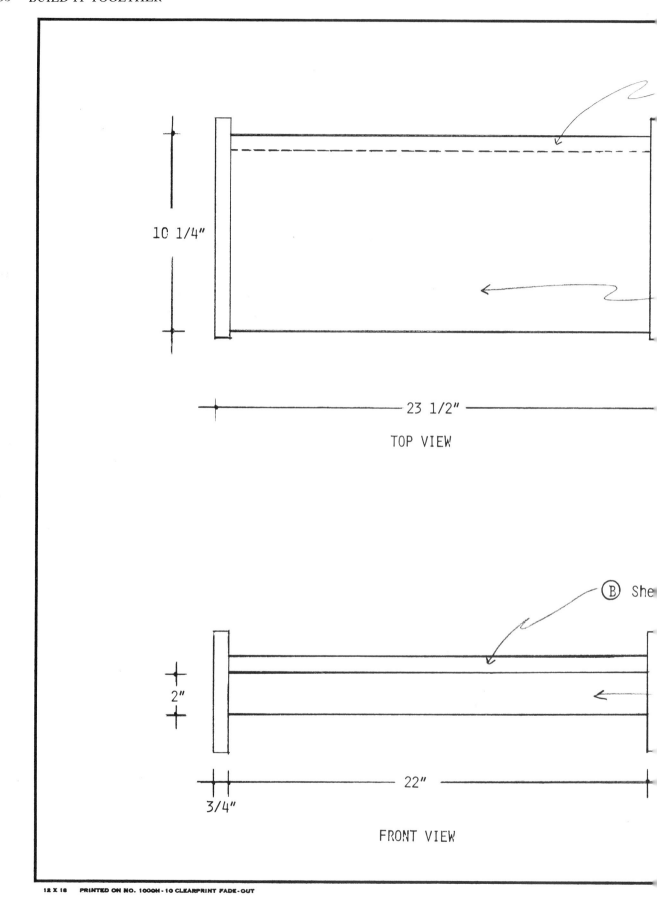

10 1/4"

23 1/2"

TOP VIEW

Ⓑ She

2"

22"

3/4"

FRONT VIEW

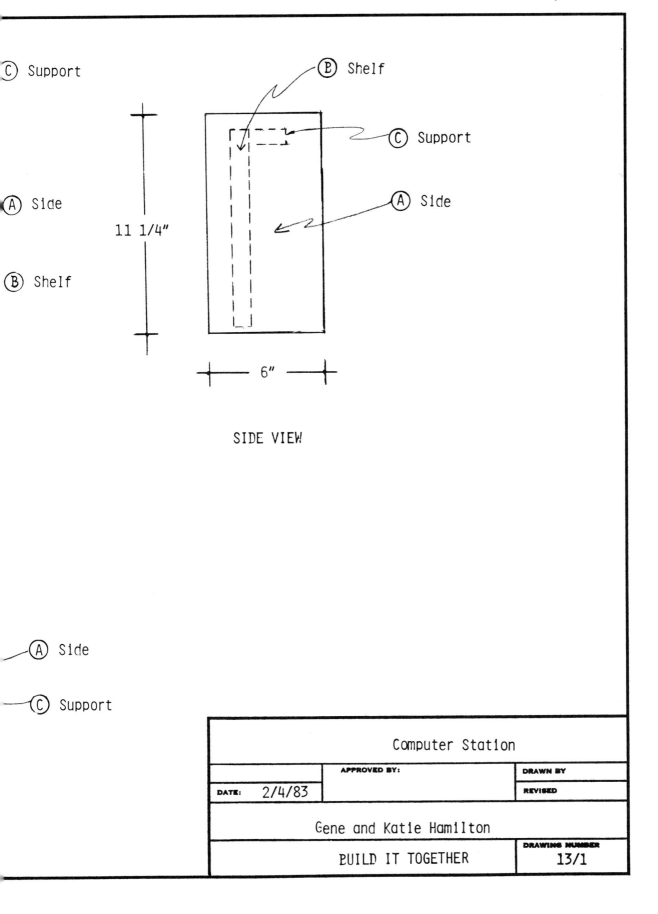

Ⓒ Support

Ⓑ Shelf

Ⓒ Support

Ⓐ Side

11 1/4"

Ⓐ Side

Ⓑ Shelf

6"

SIDE VIEW

Ⓐ Side

Ⓒ Support

Computer Station		
	APPROVED BY:	**DRAWN BY**
DATE: 2/4/83		**REVISED**
Gene and Katie Hamilton		
BUILD IT TOGETHER		**DRAWING NUMBER** 13/1

$\mathbb{B}$ook Rack

TIME REQUIRED: ¾ day (time needed for cutting, building, and assembling project; does not include drying time of glue or finish)

A cribbage board inspired our design for this nifty little desk-top book rack. Instead of pegs placed in holes to keep score, our pegs hold a movable partition in place.

We used 1″ × 8″ pine lumber, but oak or other hardwoods will make an even more handsome book rack. Just like craftsmen of past generations, you'll make your own doweling jig to help you drill holes for the base and partition pegs. This jig aligns the peg holes in the movable partition and base. The sides of the rack are strengthened with the addition of glue blocks under the bottom piece.

All the parts are cut from one 1″ × 8″ pine stock. Lay out the measurements for the ends (A), bottom (B), and movable partition (C) on the pine, following the Cutting List. Cut the jig from scrap.

The guide holes on the jig are laid out first. Use a tape measure and pencil to make marks along its long edge 1¼″ from each end and in the center 3⅝″ from each end. Use a square to draw straight lines through these marks across the jig.

Find the center of the jig ends by measuring 1½″ from either side, and make a mark on the ends. Use the square to draw a straight line through this mark down the center of the jig. Three **X**s are formed, marking the location of the guide holes. Use a drill with a ⅜″ bit to bore these holes. One team member should check that the drill is held square to the jig to make sure the holes are straight.

Mark the location of the peg holes on the bottom of the rack on its edge. Measure 4″ from the end of the bottom piece, and use your square to draw a straight line across the bottom. Repeat on the other end, and then mark off lines at 2″ intervals between these layout lines. Draw lines across the bottom at the 2″ intervals.

You are now ready to drill peg holes in the bottom. Align the holes of the jig with one of the layout lines, and clamp the jig to the bottom. Check to see that the end of the jig is flush with the sides of the bottom, then drill three ⅜″ holes through the bottom, using the holes in the jig as your guide.

Remove the jig, align the holes over another

layout line, clamp it to the bottom, and repeat the drilling. Carefully check the jig alignment before each drilling, and your movable partition pegs will fit exactly.

After you have drilled all twelve peg holes in the bottom, your jig is nailed to a piece of scrap to form a doweling guide. Nail the scrap to the jig with number 6 finishing nails. Align the scrap piece so that the jig holes are positioned over the center of the bottom of the movable partition (C). When your doweling jig is complete, position it on the end of the partition so that its end is flush with the side of the partition. Clamp the jig into place, then drill ⅜″ holes, 1″ deep, in the end of the partition, using the jig to guide you. Have one member check that the drill is held straight.

Remove your jig, and put a drop of glue on the end of a ⅜″ dowel. Tap it into a hole in the partition. Glue the other dowels in place the same way.

The ends are held to the bottom with four number 6 finishing nails and glue. Lay out the position of the nails by measuring up 1⅛″ from the bottom of the ends and using the square to draw a straight line across both ends. On the inner sides of the ends, draw another line ¾″ from the bottom to help you align the ends with the bottom when you attach them. Then drive four evenly spaced number 6 finishing nails along the line 1⅛″ from the bottom of each end.

Put glue on one end of the bottom (B), and place one end (A) in position so that the nails are centered over the side. Use the layout lines you drew ¾″ from the bottom on the inner side of the end as a guide. Have one team member hold the pieces in position while the other drives nails. Then glue and nail up the other side. Use a nail set to sink the nailheads below the surface of the wood.

Cut two small pieces of scrap about ½″ × ¾″ × 3″. Glue these blocks to the underside of the bottom in the joint between the bottom and the end.

Sand all corners smooth with number 120 sandpaper. If the partition pegs fit too tight in the base, take your ⅜″ drill and work it back and forth in the holes to enlarge them.

Our book rack is finished with a light-colored Puritan Pine stain. We also gave it a coat of paste wax for long-lasting protection.

SHOPPING LIST

Item	Quantity
1″ × 8″ clear pine	5′
⅜″ hardwood dowel	1′
number 6 finishing nails	small box
wood glue	6-ounce bottle
number 120 sandpaper	2 sheets
finish	1 pint

CUTTING LIST

Part	Name	Quantity	Size	Material
A	end	2	¾″ × 7¼″ × 9″	1″ × 8″ pine
B	bottom	1	¾″ × 7¼″ × 14″	1″ × 8″ pine
C	partition	1	¾″ × 7¼″ × 4″	1″ × 8″ pine
D	dowel	3	⅜″ × 1¼″	hardwood dowel
E	doweling jig	1	¾″ × 7¼″ × 3″	1″ × 8″ pine

Lay out the guide holes in the doweling jig (E) by drawing lines across its long edge 1¼″ from each end and, in the center, 3⅝″ from either end. Then draw a lengthwise line through the center of the jig.

Drill three ⅜″ holes through the jig at the layout marks.

To finish your doweling jig, nail it to a piece of scrap so that the holes are centered over the end of the partition (C).

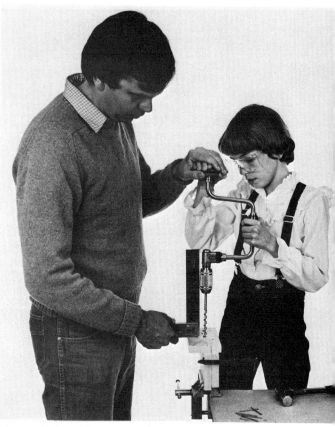

Clamp the doweling jig to the partition, aligning it flush with the edge of the partition, and then drill ⅜" holes.

Drive four evenly spaced number 6 finishing nails through the layout line you drew 1⅛" from the bottom of each end (A).

Put glue on the end of the bottom, and nail on the ends. Keep the ends aligned with the layout lines you drew on their inner sides ¾″ from the bottom of the piece.

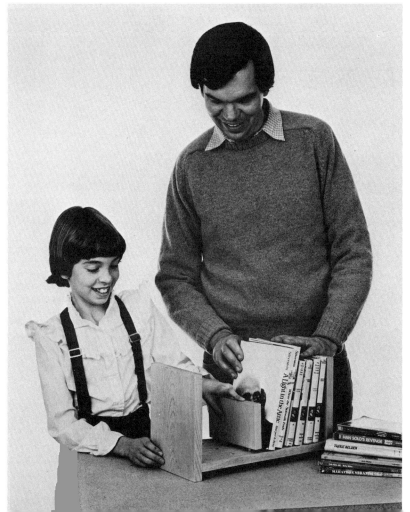

Finished book rack.

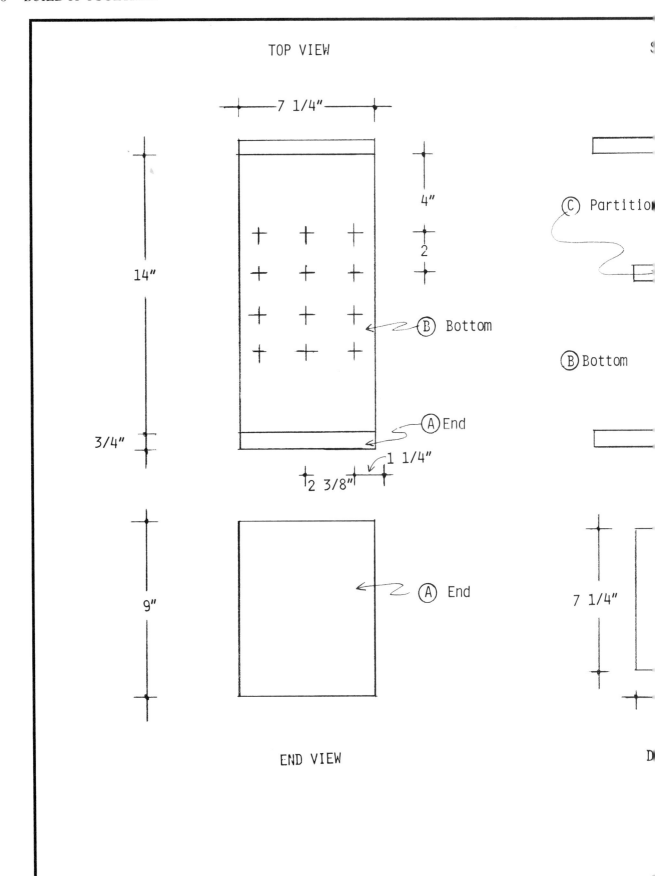

TOP VIEW

7 1/4"

14"

4"

2

B Bottom

3/4"

A End

1 1/4"

2 3/8"

A End

9"

END VIEW

C Partitio

B Bottom

7 1/4"

D

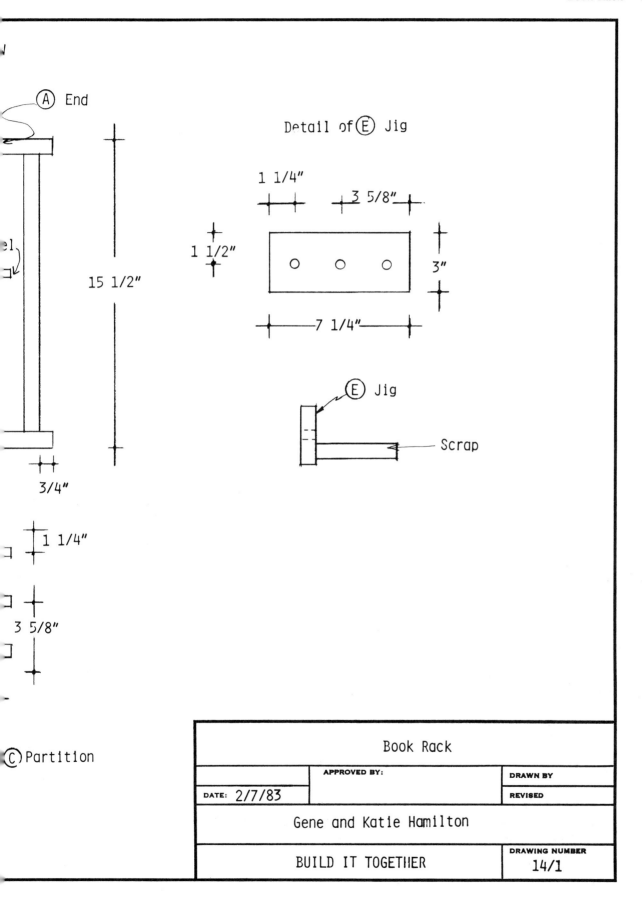

(A) End

(C) Partition

Detail of (E) Jig

1 1/4"

3 5/8"

1 1/2"

3"

7 1/4"

15 1/2"

3/4"

1 1/4"

3 5/8"

(E) Jig

Scrap

	Book Rack	
	APPROVED BY:	DRAWN BY
DATE: 2/7/83		REVISED
	Gene and Katie Hamilton	
	BUILD IT TOGETHER	DRAWING NUMBER 14/1

Collector's Briefcase

TIME REQUIRED: whole day (time needed for cutting, building, and assembling project; does not include drying time of glue or finish)

A prized collection of miniature cars, ceramic horses, or any other treasured items can be protected and showcased in our briefcase. We used inexpensive acrylic window panels for the sides so you can see your collectibles from all angles.

Although small, this project requires considerable time because many small pieces must be cut and assembled. But your time will be well-spent because you'll have a lasting showcase for any important collection. And the showcase is portable so you can carry it around with you.

We sized the briefcase for Hot Wheels or Matchbox cars, but you can change the size of the spacers, adjusting the height of shelves to accommodate just about any small collectible. You can also cut more spacers and position them to make compartments for each of your treasures.

Cutting spacers and trim pieces will take as much time as the actual assembly. Begin by cutting the $1'' \times 4''$ pine stock into two $14''$-long pieces for the top (A) and bottom (B). Then lay out a $2''$ width on the piece that will be used for the bottom, and clamp a straight piece of scrap along this line to help guide your saw as you cut B to width. Do the same for A, only cut it $1\frac{7}{8}''$ wide to allow clearance for the movable acrylic front pane.

The sides (C) are cut from $2''$-wide lattice. Use a wood miter box to ensure square cuts. Measure their length according to the Cutting List, and cut them to size. Your shelves are cut from lattice $1\frac{3}{4}''$ wide. Measure them, and cut to size, following the Cutting List.

Since there are eight spacers (E) all the same size, use a stop block to help cut the pieces. Place a scrap of wood $1\frac{1}{2}''$ from the cutting slot of the miter box, and clamp it to your table or miter box. Then push the $1\frac{3}{4}''$ lattice down the miter box until it hits, stop, and make your cut. Keep pushing the lattice along until it stops, cut, and go on. While one carpenter is cutting, the other can be sanding the parts.

Cut the top trim (F) and side trim (G) to length from $1''$-wide lattice. Don't cut the bottom trim (H) to length yet.

Your local hardware store will cut acrylic panes (I and J) for you, or you can purchase a standard-size panel large enough to cut both from. Acrylic may be scored with a sharp knife and then carefully cracked along the score line.

After all this cutting, the assembly is easy. Put glue on one end of the top (A), and nail the side (C) flush with the top and even with its back. The side will extend beyond the top at the front because the side is wider than the top. Use ⅞″ × 18 wire brads for nails, and place them back from the edges of the sides to prevent splitting. Repeat for the bottom (B).

Turn the case over, and glue and nail up the other side. Be sure to align the top and side as you did on the other end. Remember that the top is narrower than the sides.

First glue and nail the top and side trim (F and G) in place with ⅞″ × 18 wire brads on the back of the case. Align the trim pieces flush with the sides and square at the ends. When nailing on the side trim, take care to drive the nails in carefully to avoid splitting the narrow side piece.

Measure the distance between the side trim pieces to get an exact fit for the bottom trim (H). Cut it to this measurement. Nail and glue into place. Then sink all nailheads with a nail set.

Turn the case over, and insert the back pane (J) into the case. Your spacers and shelves go in next. Put a drop of glue on the back of a spacer and place it snugly against the inside and bottom of the case; place another spacer in the opposite corner. All spacers and shelves are ⅛″ short of the front edge of the sides, to leave room for the sliding front pane.

Put the first shelf in place, pushing it down against the spacers. Glue up two more spacers, and place them tightly against the inside and top of the first shelf to hold it in place. Then insert the next shelf, and repeat for all spacers and shelves. Place a small amount of glue on the ends of the top shelf and push it into place; it doesn't need a spacer above it.

The front trim is glued and nailed into place the same way as the back trim. The top trim is only glued to the front edge of the side, leaving the ⅛″ gap behind it for the front pane to slide into.

We used a modern-style drawer pull for a handle, but you can choose whatever suits your taste. Drill holes for your handle according to installation instructions furnished by the manufacturer.

A natural finish of tung oil is used to highlight the pine. If you decide to stain your case, apply sealer to the end grain of the pine, or else those parts will absorb more stain than the sides and turn out much darker.

SHOPPING LIST

Item	Quantity
1″ × 4″ pine	3′
2″-wide lattice	3′
1″-wide lattice	10′
1¾″-wide lattice	10′
⅛″ acrylic window pane	14″ × 20″
drawer pull	1
⅞″ × 18 wire brads	small box
number 120 sandpaper	2 sheets
wood glue	6-ounce bottle
finish	1 pint

CUTTING LIST

Part	Name	Quantity	Size	Material
A	top	1	¾″ × 1⅞″ × 14″	pine
B	bottom	1	¾″ × 2″ × 14″	pine
C	side	2	¼″ × 2″ × 10″	pine lattice
D	shelf	4	¼″ × 1¾″ × 14″	pine lattice
E	spacers	8	¼″ × 1¾″ × 1½″	pine lattice
F	top trim	2	¼″ × 1″ × 14½″	pine lattice
G	side trim	2	¼″ × 1″ × 9″	pine lattice
H	bottom trim	2	¼″ × 1″ × 12½″	pine lattice
I	front pane	1	⅛″ × 9¼″ × 14″	acrylic
J	back pane	1	⅛″ × 8½″ × 14″	acrylic

Clamp a straight piece of scrap to guide your saw when cutting the top (A) and bottom (B) to width.

Clamp a piece of scrap 1½" from the cutting slot of your miter box. Cut spacers (E) to length by sliding the 1¾" wide lattice down until it hits the stop.

Glue and nail the sides (C) to the bottom (H) with ⅛″ × 18 wire brads. Note that the sides are flush with the back edge of the top; there is a ⅛″ space at front.

Glue and nail the front and side trim pieces (F and G) to the back of the case. (The back is the side without the ⅛″ gap at the top.)

Place the acrylic back pane (J) into the case through the front.

Install spacers with a drop of glue. Place the shelf tight against the spacer, and then place another spacer into position.

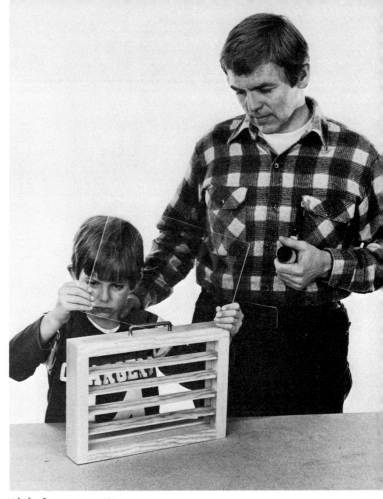

Slide front pane (I) into position.

Finished collector's briefcase.

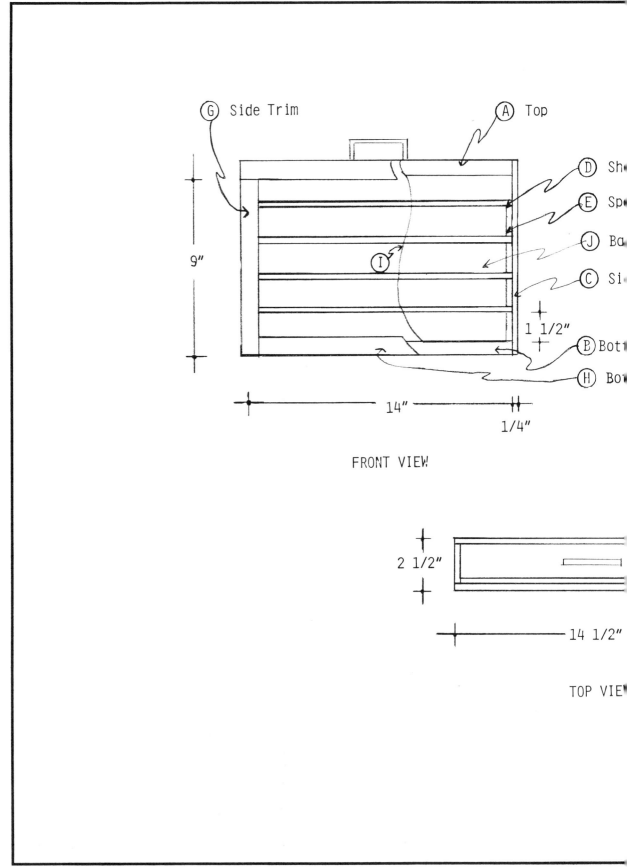

Ⓖ Side Trim

Ⓐ Top

Ⓓ Sh

Ⓔ Sp

Ⓙ Ba

Ⓒ Si

9"

Ⓘ

1 1/2"

Ⓑ Bott

Ⓗ Bo

14"

1/4"

FRONT VIEW

2 1/2"

14 1/2"

TOP VIE

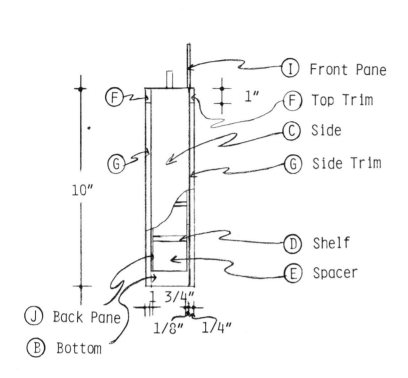

I — Front Pane
F — Top Trim
C — Side
G — Side Trim
D — Shelf
E — Spacer

1"

10"

1 3/4"

J — Back Pane
1/8"   1/4"
B — Bottom

SIDE VIEW

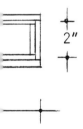

2"

	Collector's Briefcase	
	APPROVED BY:	DRAWN BY
DATE: 2/5/83		REVISED 9·01·83
	Gene and Katie Hamilton	
	BUILD IT TOGETHER	DRAWING NUMBER 15/1

$\mathbb{B}$ottle Rack

TIME REQUIRED: half day (time needed for cutting, building, and assembling project; does not include drying time of glue or finish)

In the kitchen, it organizes spice bottles; on the bathroom counter, it stores pills and toiletries. This handy little bottle rack has a thousand uses around the house. It's designed to stand alone or be mounted on a wall.

We used scrap flakeboard with lattice sides and painted our bottle rack with several coats of high gloss enamel. Plywood will work just as well, or you can use a piece of 1″ × 12″ lumber for the back. Materials for this bottle rack are inexpensive, and it makes a useful and attractive gift because it's so versatile and quick to make.

Cut the shelves (B) from a short piece of 1″ × 4″ pine. Then cut the shelf fronts (C) from 1¾″ lattice. Use an inexpensive wood miter box for a clean square cut. Cut the shelf sides (D) from the lattice, too.

Assembly is easy. Measure 6¼″ from the bottom of the back (A), and mark a straight line across its width. This is where you align the bottom edge of the top shelf. Drive four number 6 finishing nails through the back ⅜″ above its bottom edge and ⅜″ above the top-shelf layout line.

Put glue on the back edge of the bottom shelf, and have one team member hold it on the edge while the other positions it on the back. The first shelf should be aligned with the ends of the back and flush with the bottom. Nail it into place.

Glue up the back edge of the top shelf, and align its bottom edge with your layout line. Drive nails home to secure it.

The sides of the shelves (D) go on next. Check that the shelves are square with the back, and then put glue on the shelf ends. Align the sides with the front edge of the shelf, and nail them into place with ⅞″ × 18 wire brads. Place the brads as far from the edges as possible to avoid splitting the wood.

Now you glue and nail on the shelf fronts (C). Align them flush with the ends of the sides, and drive ⅞″ × 18 brads through the fronts into the ends of the sides and along the bottom edge into the shelf.

If you used plywood for the back, fill any

gaps along the edge with wood putty, and then sand your rack smooth with number 120 sandpaper.

We gave our bottle rack two coats of red enamel and planned to use it freestanding. Of course, you can paint it any color you want. Add a hanging bracket to the back if you want to mount the rack on a wall.

SHOPPING LIST

Item	Quantity
flakeboard scrap (at least 12″ × 13″)	1
1″ × 4″ pine	2′
¼″ × 1¾″ pine lattice	5′
number 6 finishing nails	2 dozen
⅞″ × 18 wire brads	small box
wood glue	small
number 120 sandpaper	2 sheets
finish	1 pint

CUTTING LIST

Part	Name	Quantity	Size	Material
A	back	1	¾″ × 12½″ × 13″	flakeboard
B	shelf	2	¾″ × 3½″ × 12″	pine 1″ × 4″
C	shelf front	2	¼″ × 1¾″ × 12½″	pine lattice
D	shelf side	4	¼″ × 1¾″ × 4¼″	pine lattice

Lay out the location of the center of the shelf (B) on the back (A) by measuring 6¼″ up from the bottom of the back. Mark this spot and another ⅜″ above it for the nail line.

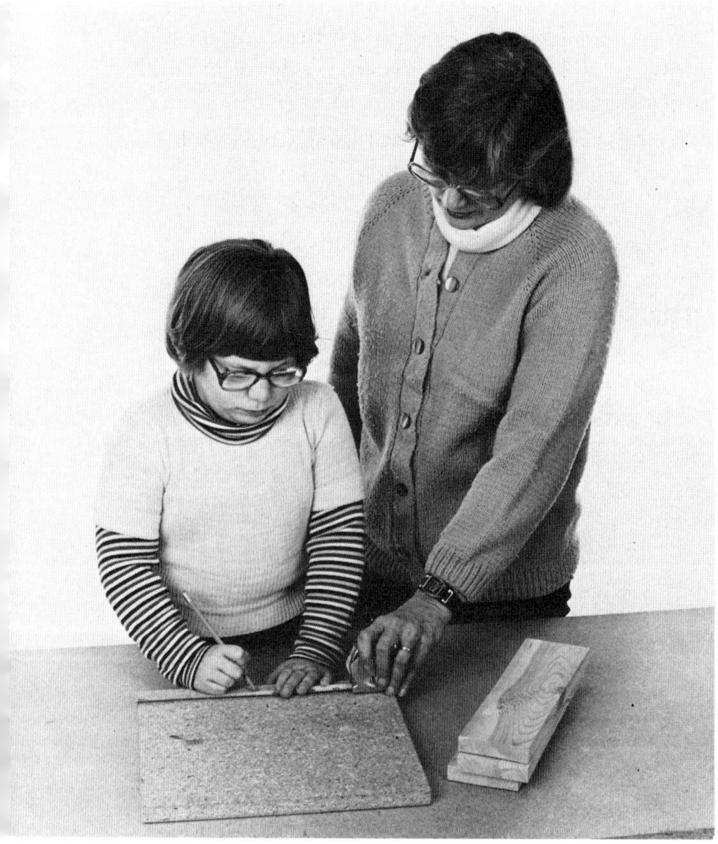

Drive four evenly spaced number 6 finishing nails ⅜″ from the bottom of the back and along nail layout line.

Apply glue to the edge of the shelf (B), and nail it in place.

Drive ⅛″ × 18 wire brads through the shelf sides (D). Locate one brad ½″ from the rear edge and another ½″ from the front edge, ¼″ from bottom.

Apply glue to the sides, and nail them into place.

Glue and nail shelf front in place with brads.

Finished bottle rack.

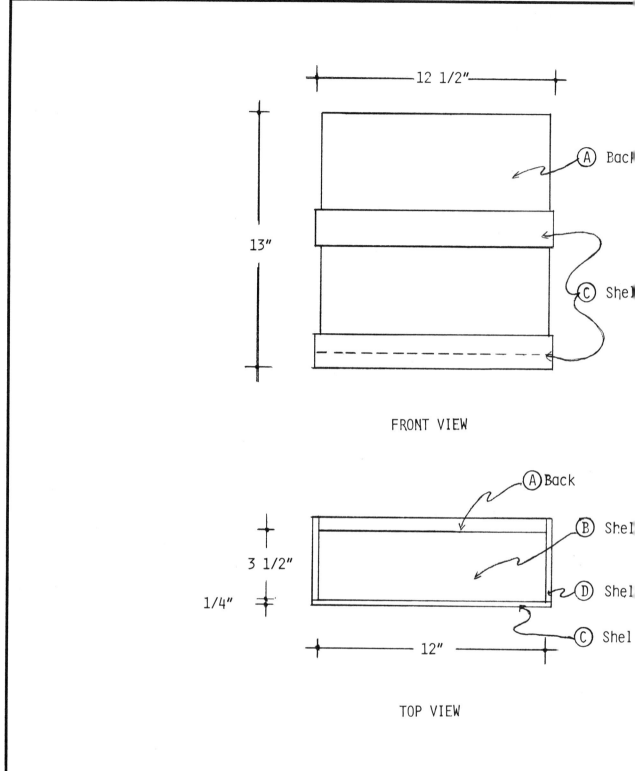

FRONT VIEW

TOP VIEW

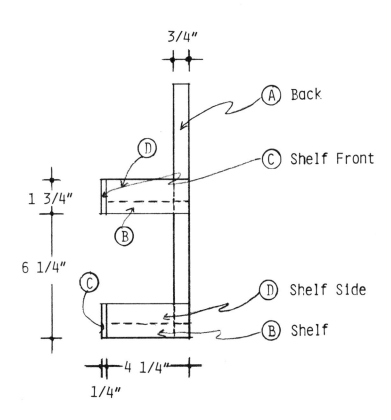

3/4"

(A) Back

(D)

(C) Shelf Front

1 3/4"

(B)

6 1/4"

(C)

(D) Shelf Side

(B) Shelf

4 1/4"

1/4"

SIDE VIEW

Bottle Rack		
	APPROVED BY:	**DRAWN BY**
DATE: 2/4/83		**REVISED**
Gene and Katie Hamilton		
BUILD IT TOGETHER	**DRAWING NUMBER**	16/1

Pet Nest

TIME REQUIRED: half day (time needed for cutting, building, and assembling project; does not include drying time of glue or finish)

Here's a great project to build for your best friend. Our drawerlike pet cradle will become the favorite snoozing spot for your cat or dog. It is made from a single 8' one-by-six and scraps of flakeboard and carpeting. The carpeting isn't tacked down so it can be removed or replaced when necessary.

The base of our pet nest is cut from a piece of 18" flakeboard shelving. If your pet needs a larger area, have the yardman at your local lumberyard cut a base from a scrap piece of flakeboard to fit your pet, and then increase the length of the sides and front and back.

Construction is fast and easy. Begin by cutting the sides (B) and front/back (C) to size, following the Cutting List. Then lay out the front door on C. Use a combination square to draw two 45-degree lines sloping 4" from the end of C. Lay out the bottom of the door by drawing a line 2½" from the top and parallel to it.

Drill a ⅜" pilot hole at the intersection of your angle lines and straight lines. If you don't have a ⅜" drill, any-size hole will do, or you may skip this step.

Cut out the door opening with a saw, then sand the edges of the opening smooth with number 120 sandpaper wrapped around a small block of wood.

Drive five evenly spaced number 4 finishing nails ⅜" from the bottom of B and C. Drive a number 4 finishing nail ⅜" from the top corner of front/back (C) to hold the front and back pieces tightly against the ends of the sides (B).

Assembly is easy. Have one team member hold the base (A) while the other runs glue down its side edge. Place the side (B) flush with the ends of the base (A), and nail it into place. Install the other side, and then glue and nail on the front and back.

113

Give your pet nest a sanding with number 120 sandpaper to round slightly any sharp corners. Then cut a piece of scrap carpet to fit the base. We made our nest a very personal home with pressure-sensitive vinyl letters.

SHOPPING LIST

Item	Quantity
1″ × 6″ pine	8′
¾″ flakeboard	cut off at least 18″ × 24″
carpet scrap	at least 18″ × 24″
wood glue	small bottle
wood putty	small can
number 4 finishing nails	small box
number 120 sandpaper	2 sheets
2″ vinyl letters	1 set

CUTTING LIST

Part	Name	Quantity	Size	Material
A	base	1	¾″ × 18″ × 24″	flakeboard
B	side	2	¾″ × 5½″ × 18″	pine
C	front/back	2	¾″ × 5½″ × 25½″	pine

Use a combination square to draw a 45-degree layout line for the entrance. Place the square 4″ from the end of C.

Drill a ⅜″ hole in C at the corner of the front door cutout.

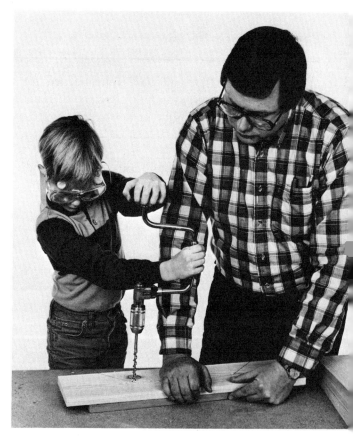

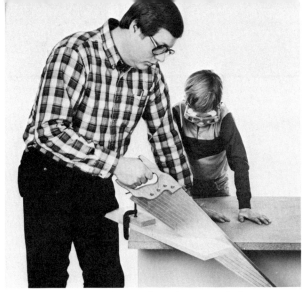

Secure C to your table with a clamp, and then cut out door.

Drive number 4 finishing nails ⅜" from the bottom of the sides (B) and front/back (C).

Glue and nail the front (C) to the base and the sides.

Use a nail set to sink nails and then fill holes with wood putty.

Finished pet nest.

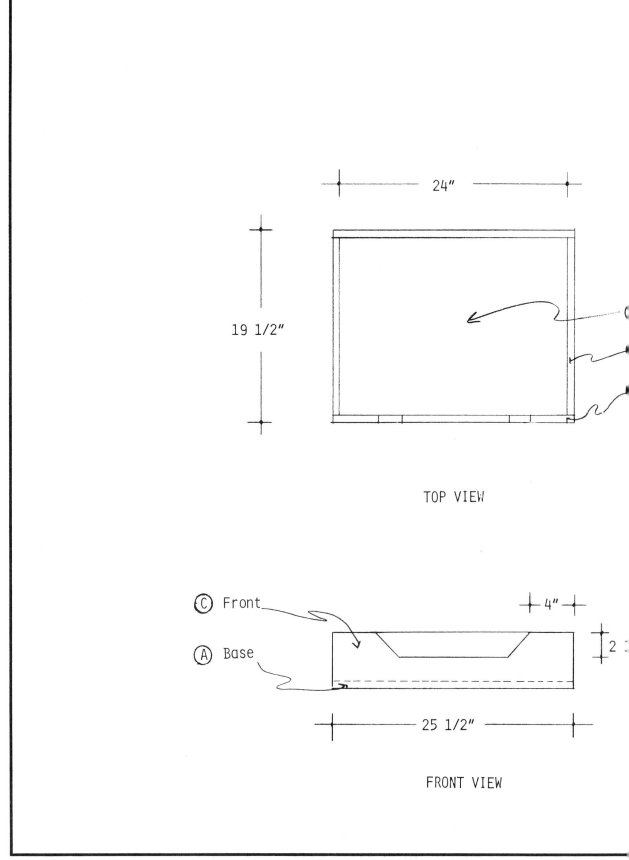

24"

19 1/2"

TOP VIEW

Ⓒ Front

Ⓐ Base

4"

25 1/2"

FRONT VIEW

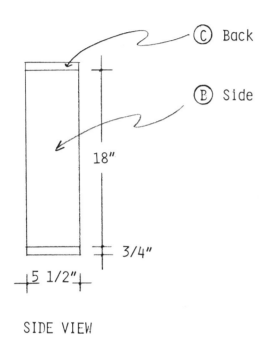

Ⓒ Back

Ⓑ Side

18"

3/4"

5 1/2"

SIDE VIEW

	PET NEST		
	APPROVED BY:		DRAWN BY
DATE: 2/19/83			REVISED
BUILD IT TOGETHER			
Gene and Katie Hamilton			DRAWING NUMBER 17/1

$\mathbb{F}$ootstool

TIME REQUIRED: half day (time needed for cutting, building, and assembling project; does not include drying time of glue or finish)

Our Shaker-style footstool combines the talents of woodworking and cord weaving. Impressive looking as it is, it is not difficult to make.

The legs are made of inexpensive 2″ × 2″ furring lumber, and eight rungs are cut from ⅞″ dowel stock. We used 6 mm. macramé cording that came in a 100-yard skein for the seat; you can choose heavy yarn, purse cording, or even heavy twine.

Construction of the stool frame is easy. Following the Cutting List, cut the legs (A) from 2″ × 2″ stock and the rungs (B) from ⅞″ dowel stock.

Next, lay out the holes for the dowels on the legs. Use a square, and draw a line across the face of the leg 1″ down from its top. Then draw another line 6″ down the leg from this line. Mark the center of these lines (¾″ from either side) to indicate the center of the rung holes. Lay out the other three legs in the same way.

The lower rung holes, located on an adjacent face, are marked out next. Before you mark these holes, pair up the legs by turning them on their sides so that the upper holes are facing one another. Make an X on the side facing up. Lay out the location of the lower holes on these sides, and you'll have matching pairs of legs. The lower rung holes are located 2⅛″ from the top of the leg, and the lower holes 6″ farther down.

Before you drill your holes, recheck that you have matching legs. Place them in position, and see that there are matching dowel holes, upper holes opposite upper holes. Then drill a ⅞″ hole 1″ deep through the layout marks. Have one member of the team check that the drill is straight.

Assembly is quick. Apply a small amount of glue to the ends of the dowels, and place them in the holes. Use a hammer and a scrap block of wood to tap the dowels until they reach the bottom of the hole. Place the stool on a flat surface, and check that all the legs touch the ground. If they don't, twist the stool into correct alignment.

After the glue has dried, sand your stool with number 120 paper, and give it several coats of tung oil.

Stringing the seat is next. Nine groups of six strands make up the pattern. Begin by tacking the taped end of the cording to a leg, just under the lower rung. Then wind fifty-four rows, or "warps," around the lower pair of rungs. When finished, you should have fifty-four strands of yarn on the top and bottom. At the end of the fifty-fourth row, pull out about 4' of cord, and cut it off. Tape one end to a pencil or craft stick, which you'll use as a weaving needle. Now you're ready to begin "wefting" the pattern. There is a top and bottom pattern. First, weave your cord through the top strands and then return it underneath, weaving it through the bottom layer.

Pull the stick and cording over the lower rung, loop it around, and then run it under the seat to the nearest upper rung. Count over six strands, and tuck the stick under the seventh. Count five more (six total) and bring the stick up and over the next six, and so on. Continue weaving above and below the groups of six strands until you reach the other side.

You should be above the last six strands. Turning the stool over, pull the cording over the high rung side and over the first six strands of cording on the underside of the stool. Continue weaving the cording above and below, alternating six strands. When you get to the other side, continue the pattern, turning the stool right side up.

After weaving your first six rows, the seventh row is the opposite of it. Run your needle below the next group of six strands, and reverse every six rows until you reach the end.

When you run out of yarn, simply tie the end to another piece of 4'-long cording. Plan your splices for the underside of the stool, and tuck the knot inside. Tack the end into a corner dowel when you're through.

SHOPPING LIST

Item	Quantity
2″ × 2″ pine	6'
⅞″ dowel	4 (3' lengths)
wood glue	6-ounce bottle
number 120 sandpaper	2 sheets
finish	1 pint
100-yard skein yarn	

CUTTING LIST

Part	Name	Quantity	Size	Material
A	legs	4	1½″ × 1½″ × 12½″	pine
B	rungs	8	⅞″ × 13½″	hardwood dowel

After marking the position of the dowel holes, set the combination so ¾″ protrudes from the end, then use it as a gauge to mark the center of the dowel.

Use a drill with a ⅛″ bit to make a hole 1″ deep for the dowels. Have one member check that the drill is straight.

Use a block of scrap wood and a hammer to seat the dowels in the holes.

Put a small amount of glue on the ends of the dowels, and insert them into the holes.

After wrapping fifty-four turns of cord around the lower rungs, begin weaving nine rows of six strands to create the pattern.

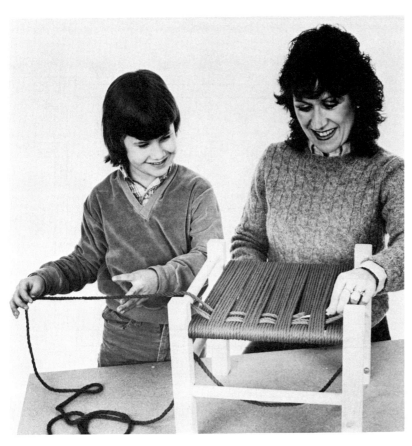

Alternate six rows of cording above and below the fifty-four strands of cording on the top and bottom of stool.

Finished footstool.

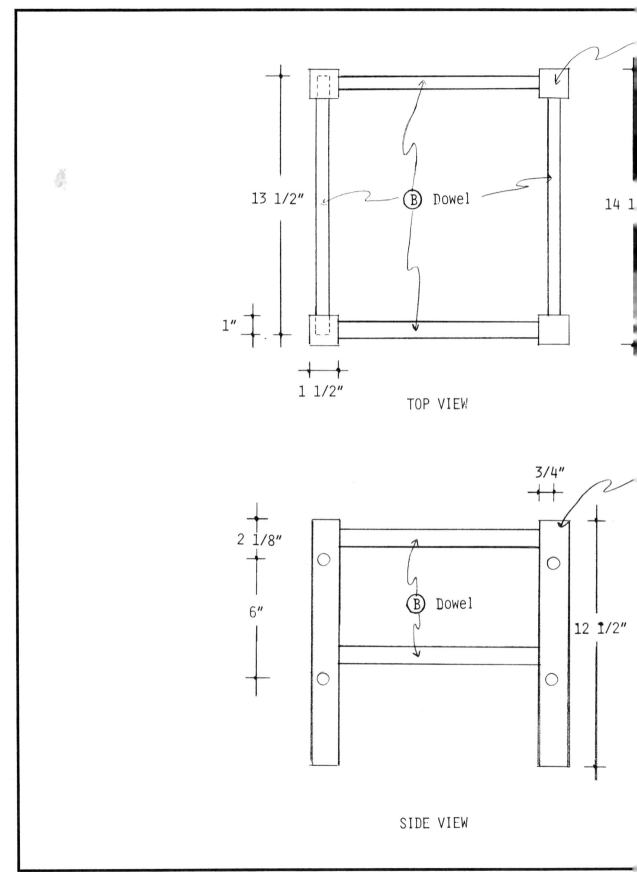

13 1/2"

(B) Dowel

14 1

1"

1 1/2"

TOP VIEW

3/4"

2 1/8"

6"

(B) Dowel

12 1/2"

SIDE VIEW

g

	FOOT STOOL		
	APPROVED BY:		**DRAWN BY**
DATE: 2/18/83			**REVISED**
	BUILD IT TOGETHER		
	Gene and Katie Hamilton	**DRAWING NUMBER** 18/1	

Napkin Holder

TIME REQUIRED: full day (time needed for cutting, building, and assembling project; does not include drying time of glue or finish)

Useful as well as good-looking, our napkin holder is crafted from solid oak. Both master craftsman and apprentice will be challenged by this project. Working with hardwoods is slightly more demanding than working with pine because all fasteners require pilot holes. Both you and your apprentice should complete another project before attempting this napkin holder.

The holder is made from scrap pieces of oak that can be purchased from your local lumberyard. If they don't have the ½″-thick stock called for to make the ends, substitute the ¾″ stock used for the base. The screw holes are filled with oak plugs; if you can't find them, buy more of the ⅜″ dowel stock used for the napkin weight, and cut your own plugs.

Begin construction by cutting the base (A) and ends (B) to size, following the Cutting List.

Sand the sides of the ends smooth, and round the edges slightly. Sand the base, but don't sand the ends where they will be glued.

Next lay out the screw holes in the ends. Locate the center of these ⅜″ holes ⅜″ from the bottom edge and ¾″ from the sides. Use a combination square to draw a line across the ends ⅜″ from bottom, then make a mark along this line ¾″ in from the side. Lay out the other ends in the same way.

Two holes are drilled through these points. First drill a ⅜″ hole ¼″ deep through your layout marks in all the end pieces. Then drill a ³⁄₁₆″ hole in the center of the larger hole completely through the ends. The larger hole holds the wood plug that conceals the screw head; the smaller hole is for the screw.

Put the ends in position aligned with the bottom edge and outside corner of the base (A). Hold it in place while one partner marks the pilot-hole location on the end of the base by making pencil marks through the holes in the ends (B).

To ensure accuracy, make small starting holes for your drill by putting the point of a nail set over your pencil marks and giving it a blow with a hammer. Then drill ⅛″-deep pilot holes through these points.

Spread glue on the ends that will be attached to the base, and put a small amount of soap on the screws to help ease them into the hard oak. Place the ends in position, and insert and tighten the number 6 × 1″ flat-headed wood screw. When the ends are in place, put a small amount of glue on the ⅜″ oak plugs, and insert them in all the screw holes. After the glue has dried, cut the plugs off close to the side.

Drill a ⅜″ hole ¾″ from the end of the napkin bar (C) in the ¾″ side. Drill another hole in the opposite end, and insert a 2″ section of doweling into each of these holes.

Give your napkin holder a thorough sanding with number 120 paper. Use sandpaper wrapped around a block of wood to sand plug stubs flush with the ends.

We gave our holder a coat of golden oak stain to highlight the grain. After the stain dried, we applied several coats of paste wax to protect the finish.

SHOPPING LIST

Item	Quantity
1″ × 8″ oak	2′
½″ × 3″ oak	2′
⅜″ hardwood dowel	1′
⅜″ oak plugs	12
number 6 × 1″ (flat-headed) wood screws	12
wood glue	small 6-ounce bottle
number 120 sandpaper	2 sheets
stain	1 pint
bar-soap sliver	

CUTTING LIST

Part	Name	Quantity	Size	Material
A	base	1	¾″ × 7″ × 7″	oak
B	ends	4	½″ × 3″ × 5½″	oak
C	bar	1	¾″ × 1″ × 9½″	oak
D	dowel	2	⅜″ × 2″	⅜″ hardwood dowel

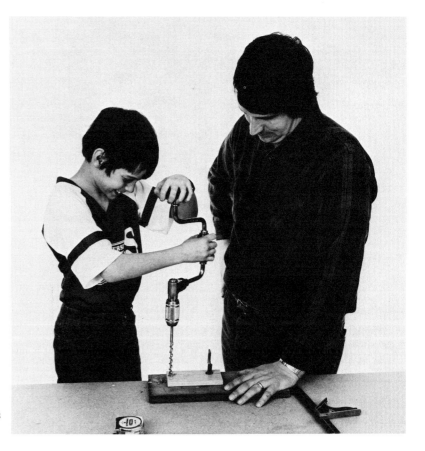

Use a ⅜″ drill to make holes ¼″ deep in the ends (B) for the screw heads.

Drill ³⁄₁₆″ holes through the center of the ³⁄₈″ holes all the way through the ends (B).

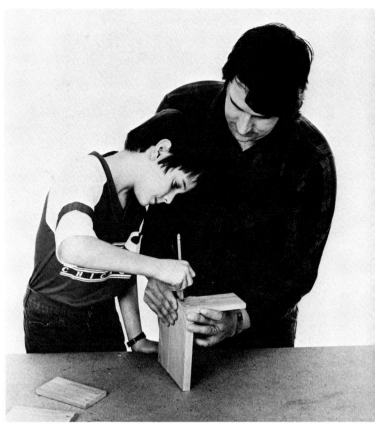

Put end (B) in position on the base (A), and mark the location of the pilot holes with a pencil placed through the holes in B.

Drill ⅛″ pilot holes for the screws in the ends of the base.

Spread glue on an end, and soap up the number 6 × 1″ flat-headed wood screws.

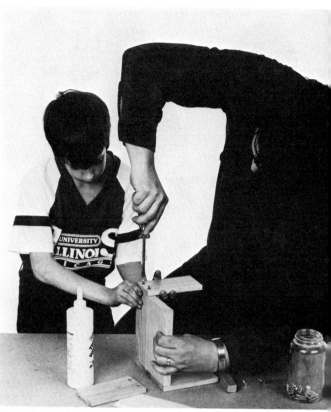

Place the end in position, and tighten the wood screws.

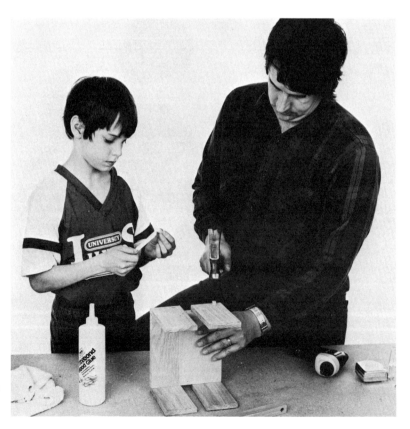

Put a small amount of glue on the plugs, and insert them in the screw holes. Tap them in place with a hammer.

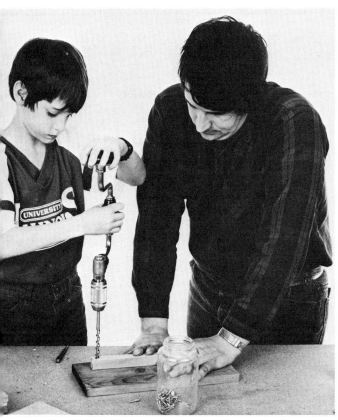

Drill a ⅜″ hole ¾″ from the end of the napkin bar (C).

Sand the napkin holder smooth with number 120 sandpaper.

Finished napkin holder.

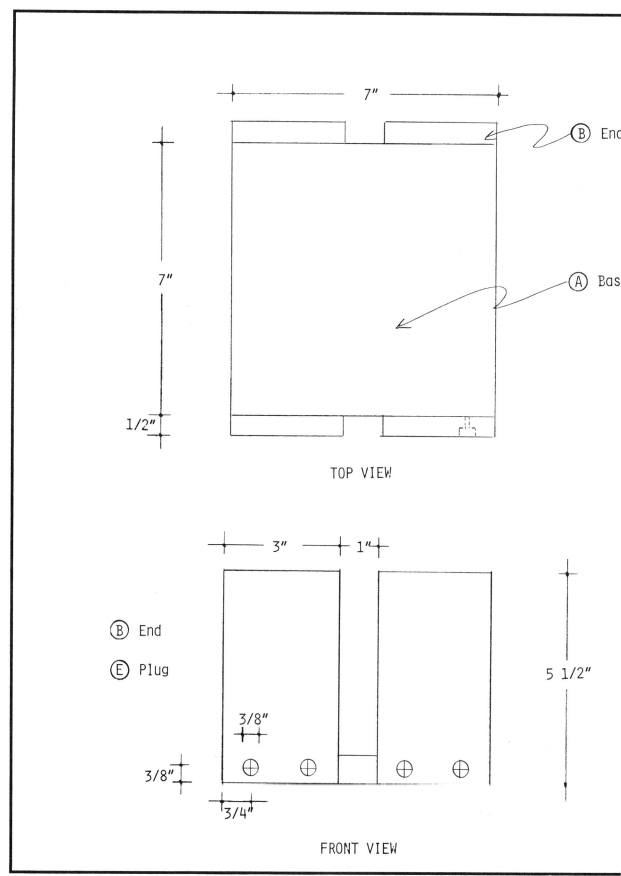

7"

7"

1/2"

(B) End

(A) Bas

TOP VIEW

3"   1"

(B) End

(E) Plug

5 1/2"

3/8"

3/8"

3/4"

FRONT VIEW

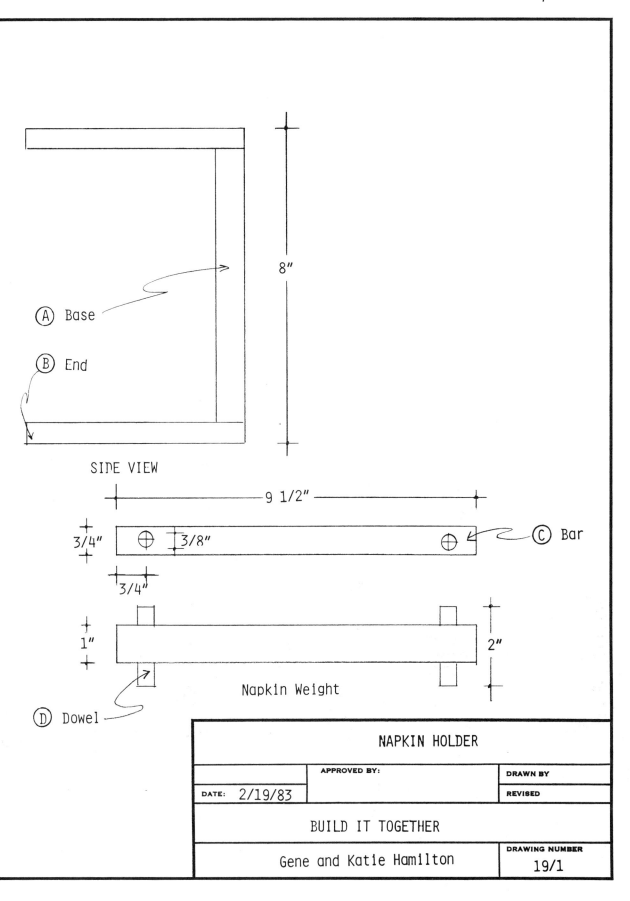

SIDE VIEW

(A) Base

(B) End

9 1/2"

3/4"

3/8"

(C) Bar

3/4"

1"

2"

8"

Napkin Weight

(D) Dowel

NAPKIN HOLDER		
	APPROVED BY:	**DRAWN BY**
DATE: 2/19/83		**REVISED**
BUILD IT TOGETHER		
Gene and Katie Hamilton		**DRAWING NUMBER** 19/1

Gift Boxes

TIME REQUIRED: half day (time needed for cutting, building, and assembling project; does not include drying time of glue or finish)

Just like the early pioneers, who made these simple basket boxes of pine with grapevine handles, we designed ours so that you can put them together easily and effortlessly. The simple construction makes these boxes ideal gifts. Fill them with candy or cookies, or use them on a dresser or dining-room table. They're popular home accessories that anyone will want.

We made the boxes in two sizes. Construction is identical; both use lattice for the sides and bottom. The larger box uses grapevine for a handle; the smaller has a braid handle made from heavy twine.

Lattice is readily available at lumber stores, but you'll have to take a walk in the woods or to a florist for the grapevine. We soaked our grapevine in warm water for several hours to make it soft and pliable to work with. Both the boxes are finished natural.

Begin construction by cutting the lattice to size. The sides and ends of both boxes are cut from 3½″-wide lattice. The bottom of the small box is formed by a single piece of 5½″-wide lattice, and the bottom of the large box is two sections of 3½″-wide lattice. For all measurements, see the Cutting List.

Lay out the location of the large box-handle holes on the sides (A), measuring 8½″ from either end. Make a pencil mark, then measure 1″ down from the top edge. Drill a ¼₆″ hole on both sides of this mark, and then do the same on the other side piece.

Drill handle holes in the ends of the small box. They are located 1″ from the side and top of the end (C). Drill a ¾₆″ hole in each corner of the two ends for the handles to slip through.

The boxes are assembled by driving two ⅞″ × 18 wire brads ⅛″ along the edges of the sides. Be careful not to split the wood. When all the nails are in place, apply glue to the ends of the sides and ends (B and C). Place the sides on top of the end, square them up, and nail them together.

Drive evenly spaced wire brads every 2″ around the edges of the bottom. Keep them ⅛″

from the edge. Then turn the boxes over, and apply glue to the edge of the sides and ends. Put the bottom in place. Have one member of the team hold it square while the other drives the brads.

When the glue is dry, sand the boxes smooth. If the ends or sides overlap slightly, place a piece of sandpaper on a flat surface, and rub the end of the box over it; this will grind down high spots and leave ends square.

If your grapevine is dry and stiff, soak it in water until it becomes pliable. Then make a loop by passing thin wire through the handle holes. Place the end of the grapevine in this loop, and pull the loop tight. Then form another loop and pull it tight. Finally, wrap the wire around the loop between the grapevine and outside the box and tie wire off.

Heavy packing twine was used as a handle for the smaller box. Take three 12"-long strands, and push them through one handle hole in the end of the small box; then tie a knot inside the box. Braid the twine, and pass the other end through the opposite hole and tie it off. Cut the strands neatly at the knots.

We gave the boxes a natural finish of Minwax. When the finish dried, we followed with a coat of paste wax for protection.

SHOPPING LIST
Both Gift Boxes

Item	Quantity
¼" × 3½" lattice	12'
¼" × 5½" lattice	1'
wood glue	small
⅞" × 18 brads	small
number 120 sandpaper	2 sheets
thin wire	small spool
heavy twine	small spool
grapevine	2'

CUTTING LIST
Small Gift Box

Part	Name	Quantity	Size	Material
A	bottom	1	¼" × 5½" × 11"	pine lattice
B	side	2	¼" × 3½" × 11"	pine lattice
C	end	2	¼" × 3½" × 5"	pine lattice

CUTTING LIST
Larger Gift Box

Part	Name	Quantity	Size	Material
A	side/bottom	4	¼" × 3½" × 17"	pine lattice
B	end	2	¼" × 3½" × 6½"	pine lattice

Lay out the position of the handle holes on the large box by making a pencil mark 8½" from the end and 1" from the top of the side (A).

Drill a ³⁄₁₆" hole for the braid handle of the smaller box 1" from end and 1" from top of the end (C).

Drive ⅛″ × 18 wire brads along the edges of the sides. Then apply glue to the edges of the ends.

Nail the sides (A) to the ends (B) of the larger box. Nail the sides (B) to the ends (C) of the small box.

Nail and glue two bottom parts to the large box and a single bottom part to the small box.

Braid the handle of heavy twine for the small box. Wrap wire around the grapevine to form the handle of the large box.

Finished gift box.

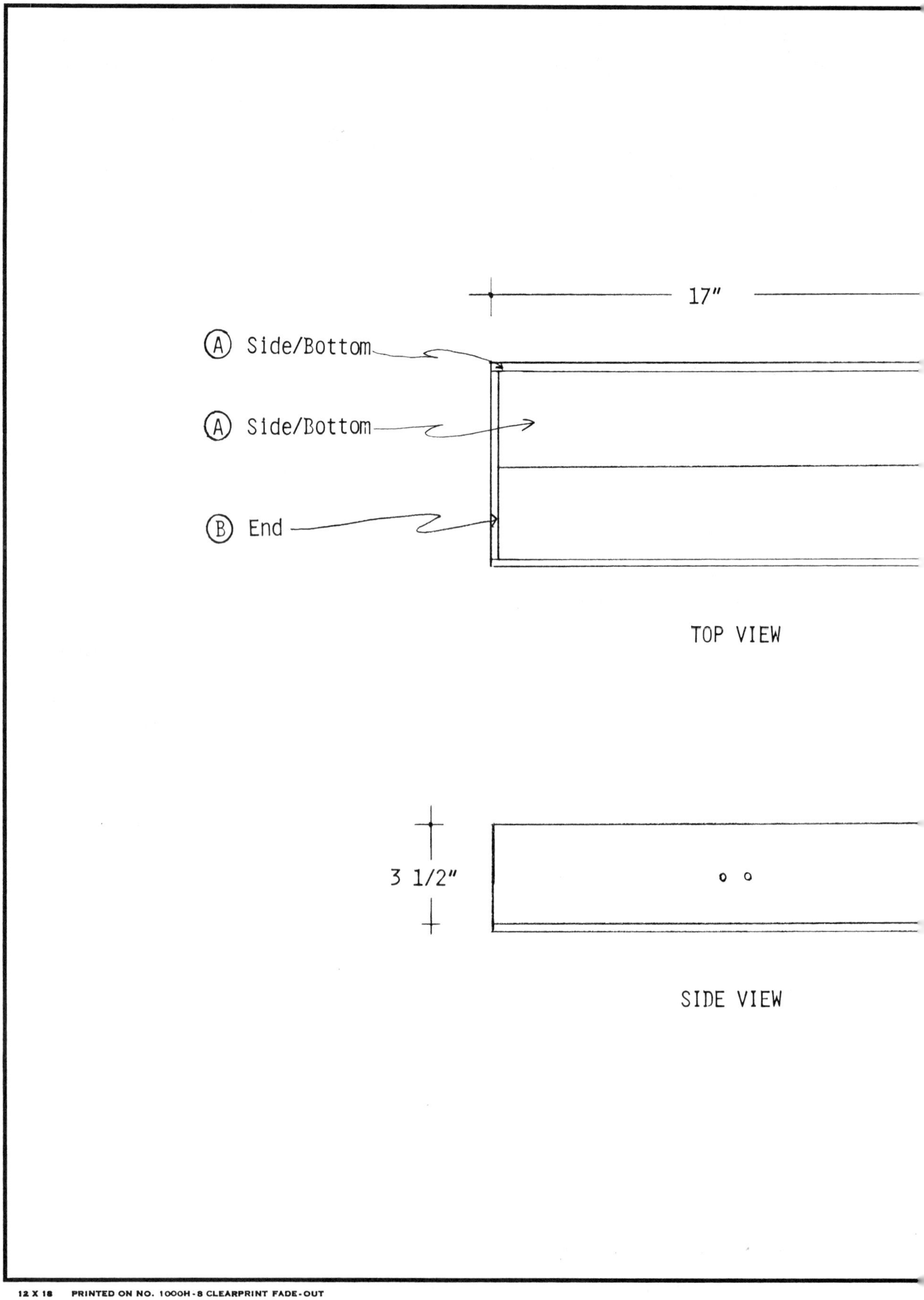
17"
(A) Side/Bottom
(A) Side/Bottom
(B) End
TOP VIEW
3 1/2"
SIDE VIEW
12 X 18 PRINTED ON NO. 1000H-8 CLEARPRINT FADE-OUT

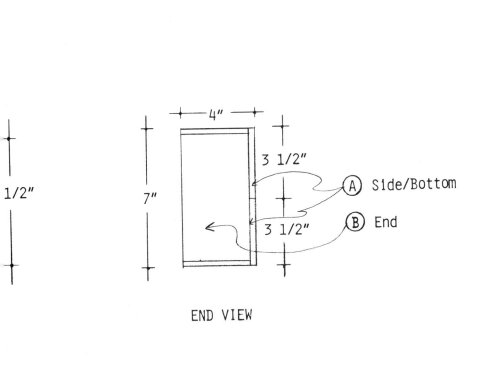

END VIEW

Large Box

Gift Boxes		
	APPROVED BY:	DRAWN BY
DATE: 2/20/83		REVISED
BUILD IT TOGETHER		
Gene and Katie Hamilton		DRAWING NUMBER 20/ 1

$\mathbb{B}$ird Feeder

TIME REQUIRED: half day (time needed for cutting, building, and assembling project; does not include drying time of glue or finish)

Here's a bird feeder sure to become a popular stopover for your feathered friends. We designed our feeder, made of redwood and acrylic windowpane, to protect the feed from rain and snow and from other critters who like to ravage a stash of food.

The feeder is filled with seed from the top, which is raised and slides up the suspension ropes. A controlled amount of seed spills out through the space below the clear pane onto the deck where the birds come to feed. When some of the seed is eaten, more will run out. With the feeder's clear sides, you can always see the seed level and refill it when needed.

Our feeder is made from redwood available at lumberyards. Since only small pieces are required, purchase scrap pieces if possible. Pine may be substituted, but it should be stained to protect it from the weather.

Cut out the full-size end pattern, and trace it on a piece of redwood. Cut this end out, and use it as a pattern for the other end. Cut the remaining pieces to length, as specified in the Cutting List.

Since redwood splits easily, use a $\frac{1}{16}''$ drill bit to make pilot holes for the nails. Drill two pilot holes along the bottom of the ends (B) and five holes $\frac{3}{8}''$ from the top edge of one top part (C).

Apply glue to the end of the bottom (F) and nail on one end with number 4 finishing nails. Turn the unit over, and glue and nail on the other end. Have one team member hold the end in position while the other does the nailing. Sink all nailheads with a nail set.

Cut acrylic sides (D) out of a piece of windowpane. Acrylic can be cut with a saw or scored with a sharp knife and then broken over a table edge. Drill three evenly spaced $\frac{1}{16}''$ holes $\frac{3}{8}''$ from the ends of the acrylic sides (D).

The side panels (D) are nailed flush with the top edge of the ends (B) with $\frac{5}{8}'' \times 18$ aluminum or brass brads. This creates a slot at the bottom for the food to pour through.

Drill two additional $\frac{3}{8}''$ holes in the base $1\frac{1}{4}''$ from the ends and in the center. Run a bead of glue down the top edge of the roof (C). Nail both

141

roof parts together with number 4 aluminum nails. You do not have to drill pilot holes in the edge of C. Turn your top over, and have one team member hold it square while the other drills a ⅜" hole in the V 1¼" from each end of the roof.

Mark the location of the feeder house on the base by measuring 1½" from each end of the base. Put glue on the bottom edges of the feeder house, and nail it to the base. You do not need pilot holes, since the nails are driven in the center of the house.

Cut a 3½' length of ⅜" rope, and tie a loop in its center. Feed the ends of the rope through the holes in the roof and the base of your feeder house. Tie a knot in the rope to hold it in place, and your feeder is ready to be filled with seed. Just lift the roof, and pour in the first meal.

SHOPPING LIST

Item	Quantity
1" × 8" redwood	1' cutoff
1" × 6" redwood	4'
⅛" acrylic windowpane	scrap (at least 8" × 12")
number 4 finishing nails (galvanized or aluminum)	small box
⅞" × 18 brads (galvanized or aluminum)	small box
wood glue	6-ounce bottle
⅜" manila rope	8'

CUTTING LIST

Part	Name	Quantity	Size	Material
A	base	1	¾" × 7¼" × 12"	redwood
B	end	2	¾" × 5½" × 6¼"	redwood
C	roof	2	¾" × 5½" × 12"	redwood
D	side	2	⅛" × 3⅜" × 12"	acrylic pane
E	rope	1	⅜" × 8'	⅜" manila rope
F	bottom	1	¾" × 2" × 7½"	redwood

Cut out the full size end pattern, and trace it on a piece of redwood.

Drill two pilot holes ⅜" from the bottom of the ends (B). Mark nail positions ⅜" from the top edge of the top (C).

Apply glue to the end of the bottom (F). Drive
number 4 finishing nails into the pilot holes drilled in
the top (C).

Hold the bottom in position while the end is nailed in
place.

Drill three ⅟₁₆″ pilot holes ⅜″ from the
edge of the acrylic side (D).

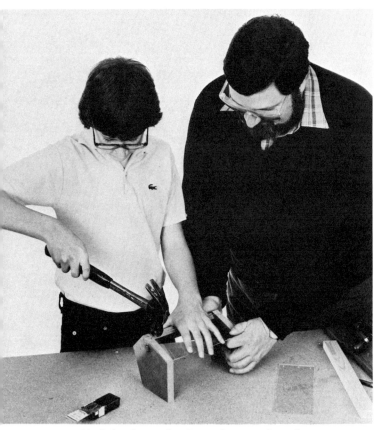

Nail the first side (D) to the top edge of the end (B) with ⅞″ × 18 brass or aluminum brads. The space at the bottom edge allows the seed to fall through.

Drill a ⅜″ hole 1¼″ from each end of the V of the top.

Glue and nail the feeder house to its base (A) with number 4 aluminum finishing nails.

Thread the ⅜″ rope through the holes in the roof and base, and knot the rope under the base.

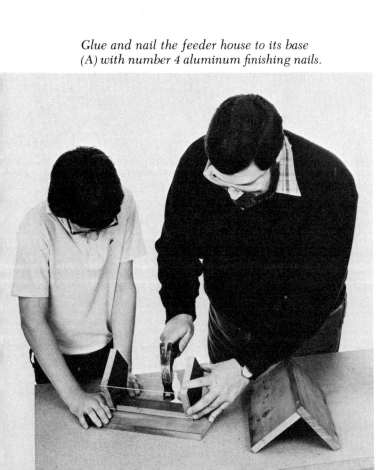

Finished bird feeder.

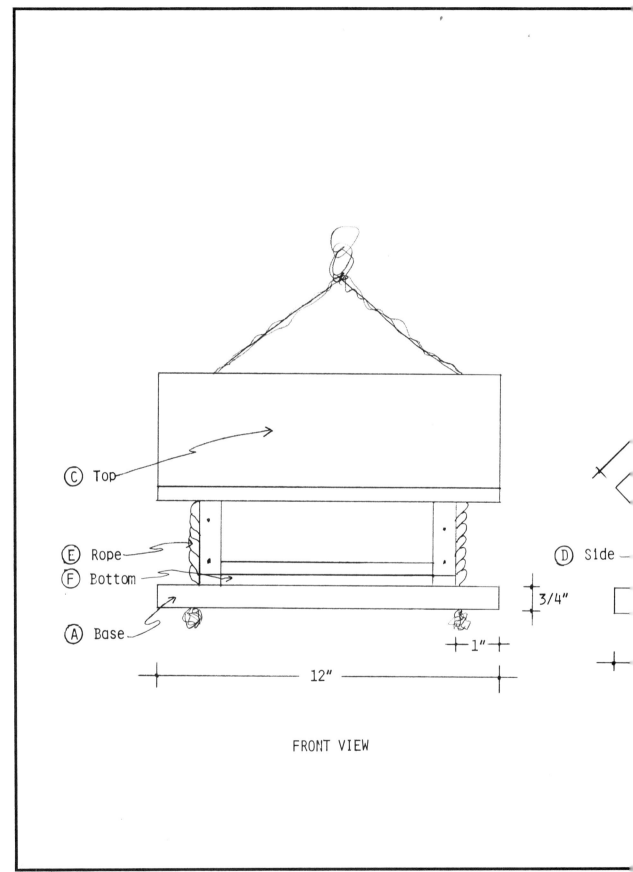

© Top

Ⓔ Rope

Ⓕ Bottom

Ⓐ Base

Ⓓ Side

3/4"

1"

12"

FRONT VIEW

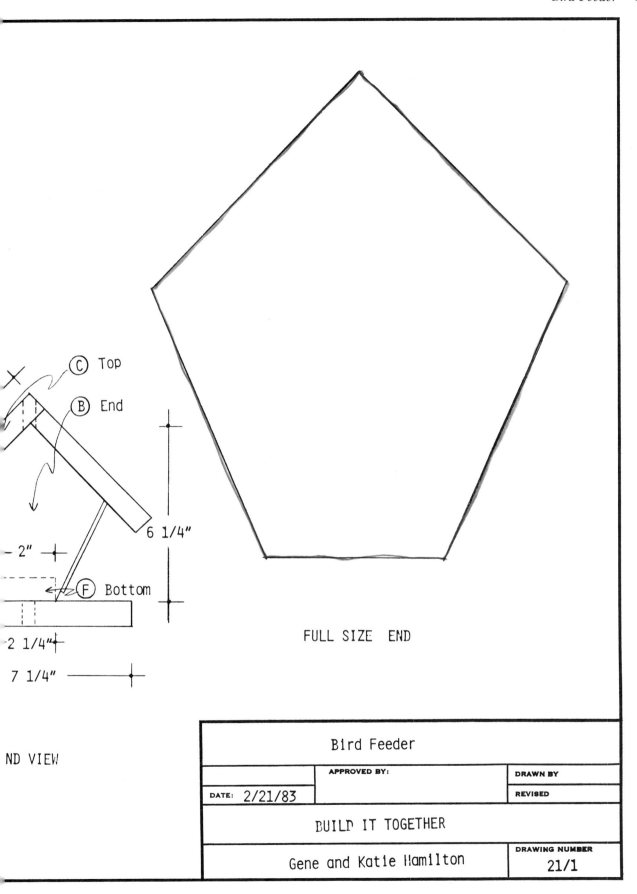

C Top

B End

6 1/4"

- 2"

F Bottom

- 2 1/4"

7 1/4"

FULL SIZE END

ND VIEW

Bird Feeder		
DATE: 2/21/83	APPROVED BY:	DRAWN BY
		REVISED
BUILD IT TOGETHER		
Gene and Katie Hamilton		DRAWING NUMBER 21/1

$\mathbb{P}$lant Center

TIME REQUIRED: almost instant (about two hours; time needed for cutting, building, and assembling project; does not include drying time of glue or finish)

The "green thumb" members of the family will proudly display their plants in this easy-to-build three-pot plant holder. We designed it around an 18″ plastic window-box liner to hold three 3″-diameter clay pots.

The planter is made of only four pieces of 1″ × 6″ wood. We chose redwood, but pine can be used. Since water spills are likely, we treated our holder with a water sealer.

Redwood is soft and easy to cut. Lay out the dimensions of the sides (A) and the top and bottom (B) on the 1″ × 6″ board, as on the Cutting List. Redwood splits easily, so use a ⅟₁₆″ drill to make pilot holes for the nails.

Choose one of your B parts for the top, and lay out the location of the pot holes. The centers are located 2¾″ from either edge, 3½″ from each end, and 9″ from either end in the center. Use a compass to draw a 1½″ radius circle at each of these points.

Then drill a ⅜″ hole inside but touching the circumference of the circle. Drill a hole in the other two circles, and then insert the blade of a coping saw through the hole. Clamp the top to the table, and cut out the pot holes.

Lay out the location of the nail pilot holes on the two sides (A). Use a combination square to draw a line across the top ⅜″ from its bottom edge. Draw another line 3⅝″ from the edge. Drill three evenly spaced ⅟₁₆″ holes along these lines.

Apply glue to the end of the bottom (B), and have one team member hold it straight while the other nails on the sides (A). Check that the lower edge of the sides is flush with the bottom.

Put glue on the end of the top (B), and nail it in place 3″ above the bottom. Then turn your holder over, and glue and nail on the other side. Set all nailheads below the surface of the wood with a nail set, and your plant holder is ready for service. Place your plastic tray on the base to catch any overflow.

We applied a coat of water sealer (Thompson's Waterseal) to help prevent water stains. This is only for appearance, since redwood is not affected by water and is naturally rot resistant.

SHOPPING LIST

Item	Quantity
1″ × 6″ redwood	5′
number 4 finishing nails	small box
wood glue	6-ounce bottle
3″ clay pot	3
4″ × 17¾″ plastic tray	1
number 120 sandpaper	2 sheets
finish	1 pint

CUTTING LIST

Part	Name	Quantity	Size	Material
A	side	2	¾″ × 5½″ × 5	·redwood
B	top/bottom	2	¾″ × 5½″ × 18″	redwood

Lay out the locations of the pot holes on the top (B) with a compass. Draw three 1½″-radius circles whose centers are located 2¾″ from either edge, 3½″ from each end, and 9″ from either end in the center of the top.

Drill a ⅜″ hole inside each circle, right of the circumference.

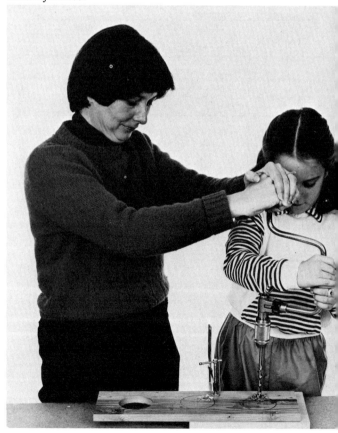

Take the blade out of a coping saw, insert it through the hole, and then reassemble the saw. Cut out the circles for the pots.

Drive number 4 finishing nails through the 1/16" pilot holes.

Put glue on the end of the bottom (B), and then nail on the sides (A).

Use a nail set to sink the nailheads below the surface of the wood.

Finished plant center.

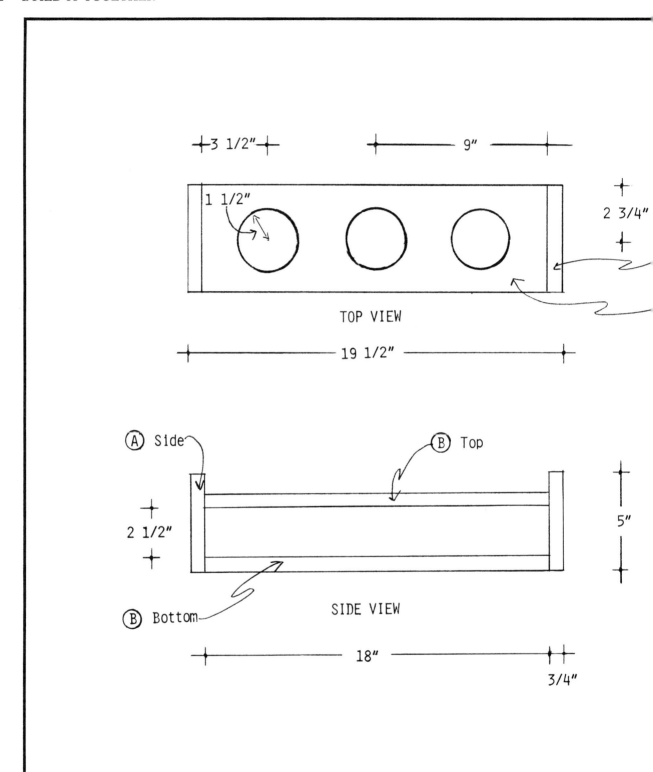

3 1/2"   9"

1 1/2"

2 3/4"

TOP VIEW

19 1/2"

(A) Side   (B) Top

2 1/2"   5"

(B) Bottom   SIDE VIEW

18"

3/4"

Side

Top

— 5 1/2" —+

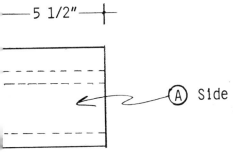

(A) Side

END VIEW

	Plant Center		
	APPROVED BY:		DRAWN BY
DATE: 3/1/83			REVISED
	BUILD IT TOGETHER		
	Gene and Katie Hamilton		DRAWING NUMBER 22/1

$\mathbb{D}$oll Slide

TIME REQUIRED: almost instant (about two hours; time needed for cutting, building, and assembling project; does not include drying time of glue or finish)

There is nothing more adorable than an almost-lifelike cuddly doll, but we noticed there's not much furniture built for them. Here is an easy-to-make slide just right for a doll 12″–20″ tall. A dowel hinge makes the slide collapsible so it can store easily when not in use.

All materials are readily available and cost next to nothing. We painted our slide a bright red; you can leave yours natural or choose a color that suits you.

Begin construction by cutting the 1″-wide lattice to length, following the Cutting List, to make the slide parts. Use an inexpensive wood miter box to make square cuts.

Drill a ⅜6″ hole through the center of the slide sides (A). With ⅝″ wire brads then glue and nail a brace to the underside of the sides at the top and bottom. Glue and nail another brace in the center of the side.

Decide which end of your slide you want to be the top. Cut the hinge dowel (F) to length, then place it across the slide frame next to the top brace. Then place the remaining brace in position next to the dowel, adjust it so the dowel has room to move, and glue and nail the brace into place.

While the slide-frame glue is drying, drill a ¼″ hole in the center of the ladder (C), 1″ from its end. Drill a ⅜6″ hole in the center of the ladder (C), 6″ down the top. Then glue and nail on the rungs (D). Place the first rung 2″ from the bottom (this is the end opposite the holes), and space the rest 2″ apart.

Glue and nail the joint brace (E) across the top braces of the slide frame. These pieces keep the dowel hinge in place.

Turn the slide frame over and apply glue to the face of the braces and along the sides. From the light cardboard cut slide bottom (G) to size, following the Cutting List, and insert it.

Your slide is easy to paint while it is in two pieces. We gave ours several coats of red spray paint, allowing it to dry between coats.

When your finish is dry, assemble the slide. Place the ¼″ dowel in the hole in the top of your ladder, and align it with the dowel slot on the underside of the slide frame. Then push the dowel into the hole. You might have to work the dowel a little since paint has probably dripped into these holes. Insert the dowel completely through the slide frame until it is flush with the other side of the ladder.

Thread string through the holes in the center of the ladder and slide sides, and tie knots in its end to keep it in place. Your slide will stand or can be folded flat for storage.

Our dolls are Brenda Lee (she's 19″) and her brother, Randy Lee (13½″). Both are Sew Sweet Dolls from Carolee Creations, 787 Industrial Dr., Elmhurst, IL 60126, toll-free telephone: (800) 323-1739 for ordering.

SHOPPING LIST

Item	Quantity
¼″ × 1″ pine lattice	15′
¼″ hardwood dowel	1′
number 120 sandpaper	2 sheets
wood glue	6-ounce bottle
⅝″ wire brads	small box
light cardboard	5½″ × 24″
light string	2′
finish or paint	½ pint

CUTTING LIST

Part	Name	Quantity	Size	Material
A	side	2	¼″ × 1″ × 24″	pine lattice
B	brace	4	¼″ × 1″ × 5½″	pine lattice
C	ladder	2	¼″ × 1″ × 18″	pine lattice
D	rung	5	¼″ × 1″ × 6″	pine lattice
E	joint brace	2	¼″ × 1″ × 2¼″	pine lattice
F	hinge dowel	1	¼″ × 6″	hardwood dowel
G	bottom	1	5″ × 24″	light cardboard

Glue and nail a brace (B) to the underside of the slide frame sides.

Nail and glue the remaining brace ¼″ from the top brace to form a channel for the hinge dowel (F).

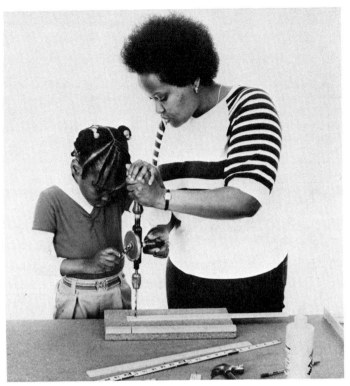

Drill a ¼" hole 1" from the end of the ladder (C) for the hinge dowel.

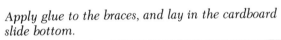

Apply glue to the braces, and lay in the cardboard slide bottom.

Nail the joint brace (E) to the bottom of the braces to form the dowel hinge hole. Give the wood a sanding with number 120 paper.

Finished doll slide.

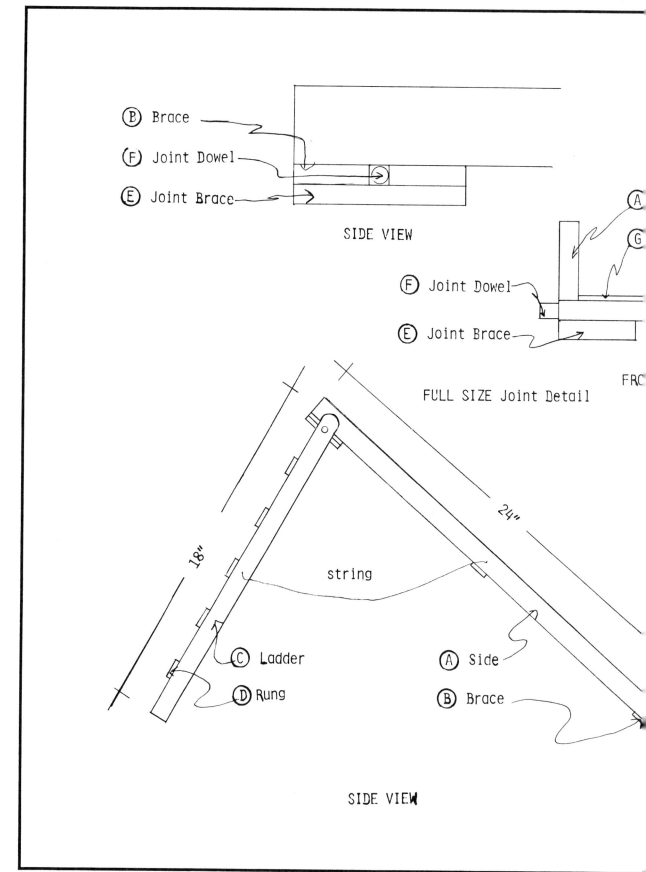

B Brace

F Joint Dowel

E Joint Brace

SIDE VIEW

F Joint Dowel

E Joint Brace

A

G

FRO

FULL SIZE Joint Detail

24"

18"

string

C Ladder

D Rung

A Side

B Brace

SIDE VIEW

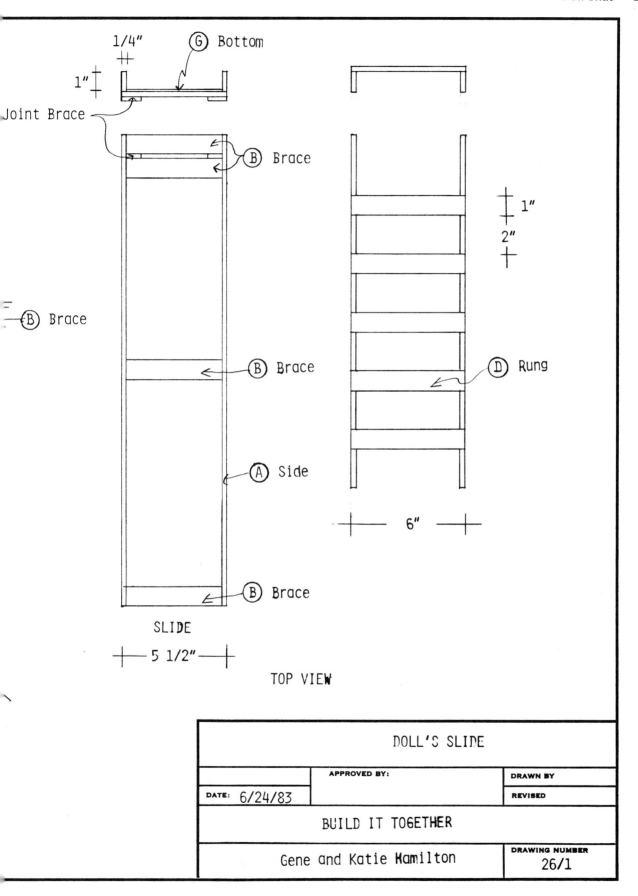

1/4"

Ⓖ Bottom

1"

Joint Brace

Ⓑ Brace

Ⓑ Brace

Ⓑ Brace

Ⓐ Side

SLIDE

5 1/2"

TOP VIEW

1"

2"

Ⓓ Rung

6"

	DOLL'S SLIDE	
DATE: 6/24/83	APPROVED BY:	DRAWN BY
		REVISED
	BUILD IT TOGETHER	
Gene and Katie Hamilton		DRAWING NUMBER 26/1

ℝecord Rack

TIME REQUIRED: half day (time needed for cutting, building, and assembling project; does not include drying time of glue or finish)

This contemporary-looking record rack will compliment a den or bedroom and solve the problem of storing those cumbersome record albums or piles of magazines. It's not only good-looking but simple to build using dimensional lumber from a home center or lumberyard. One 3′ piece of 1″ × 12″ lumber and some 1″ lattice strips are all that is needed to construct our rack. We made ours portable by adding furniture casters.

Construction is fast. Cut the 1″ × 12″ into three parts for the two sides (A) and bottom (B), following the dimensions on the Cutting List. Then cut the 1″ lattice into the lengths required. Use an inexpensive miter box, and clamp a piece of scrap 14¼″ from the cutting slot to act as a stop when cutting the slats. Slide the lattice through the miter box until it hits the stop, then cut it to length. This saves time, since you will not have to measure each piece.

Lay out the location of the nails with a combination square. Draw a line ⅜″ from the bottom of the sides. Then drive four evenly spaced number 4 finishing nails along this line. Drive a ⅞″ × 18 finishing nail into the ends of each slat (C) about ⅜″ from its end. Now you are ready to assemble your rack.

Run a bead of glue down the edge of the bottom (B). One member of the team should hold the bottom upright while the other nails the sides into place.

Turn your rack on its side. Put a little glue on the end of a slat, and nail it into place flush with the top edge of the sides. Do the same on the other side, then check that the rack sides are square.

Glue and nail on the bottom slat, then use a piece of scrap lattice as a spacer when placing the remaining slats in position. Adjust the position on the last slat visually.

To add casters to your rack, turn it over, and follow the manufacturer's direction for installation. Locate the casters about ¾″ from the front and side of the rack. The type we purchased requires four screws. Put the caster in place, and mark the location of the screws. Remove the caster, and drill a

⅟16″ pilot hole for each screw. Replace the caster, and screw it in place.

We finished our rack naturally by giving it a coat of wipe-on finish. If you want a more colorful rack, paint it with two coats of high-gloss enamel. If you don't have records to store, use your rack to hold magazines.

SHOPPING LIST

Item	Quantity
1″ × 2″ pine	4′
1″ pine lattice	20′
number 4 finishing nails	small box
⅞″ × 18 wire brads	small box
wood glue	6-ounce bottle
ball casters	4
number 120 sandpaper	2 sheets
finish	1 pint

CUTTING LIST

Part	Name	Quantity	Size	Material
A	side	2	¾″ × 11¼″ × 11″	1″ × 12″ pine
B	bottom	1	¾″ × 11¼″ × 13″	1″ × 12″ pine
C	slat	12	¼″ × 1″ × 14¼″	pine lattice

Mark a straight line ⅜″ from the bottom of each side (A).

Evenly space number 4 finishing nails along the layout lines on the sides (A).

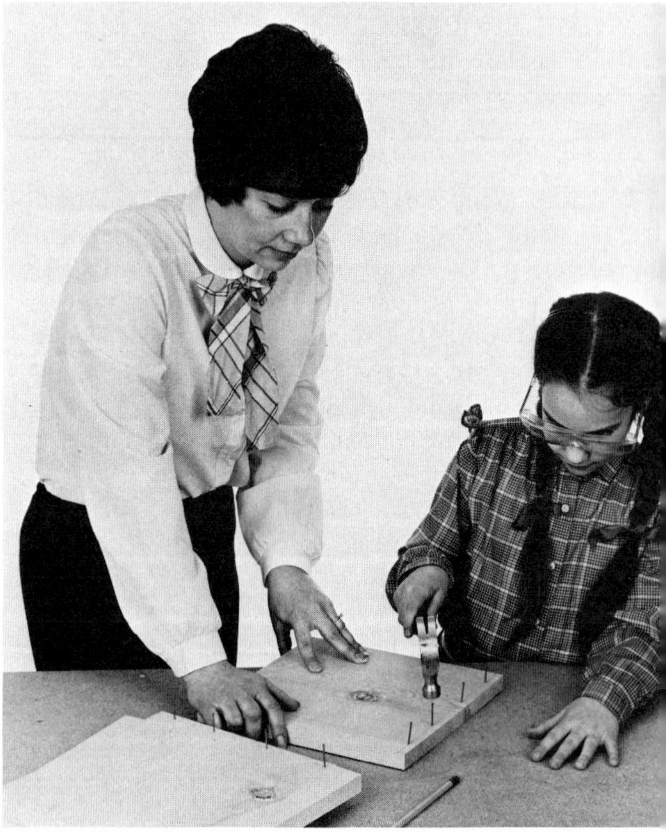

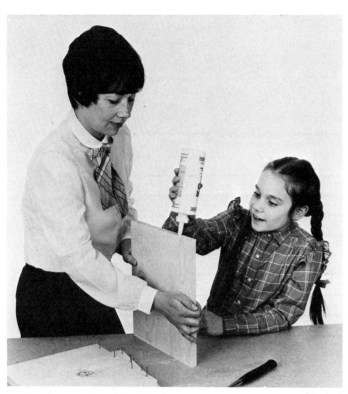

Apply glue to the end of the bottom (B).

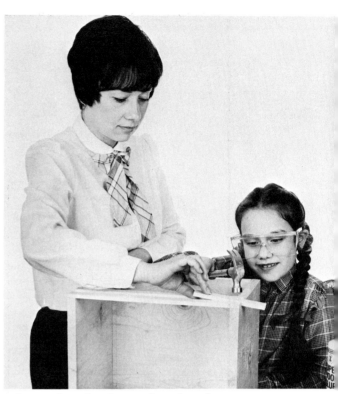

When nailing the slats to the sides, place a piece of 1" scrap lattice between the slats (C) to act as a spacer.

Drill pilot holes for each of the caster mounting screws, and screw in casters.

Finished record rack.

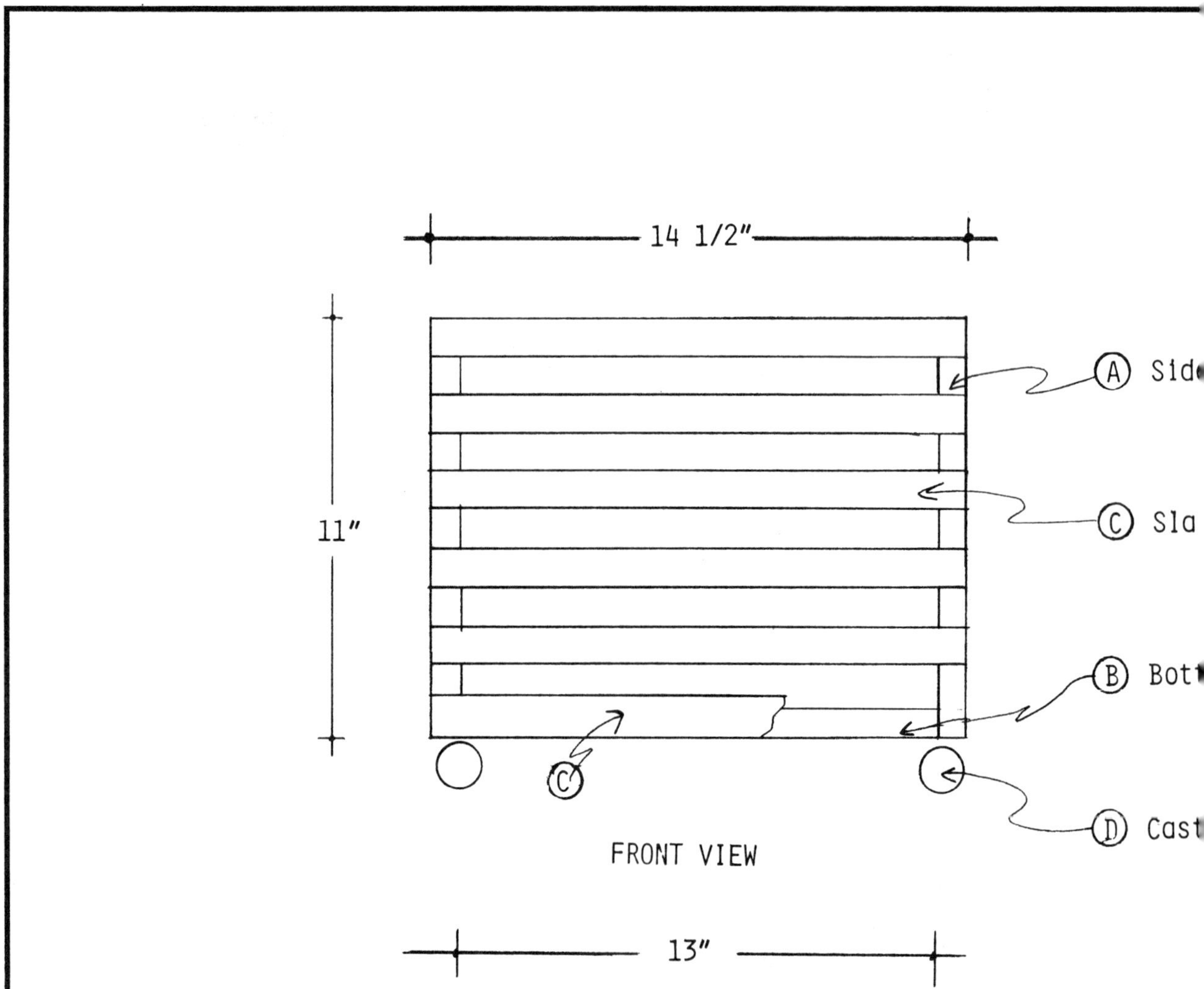

14 1/2"

11"

(A) Side

(C) Sla

(B) Bot

(C)

(D) Cast

FRONT VIEW

13"

(B) Bot

TOP VIEW

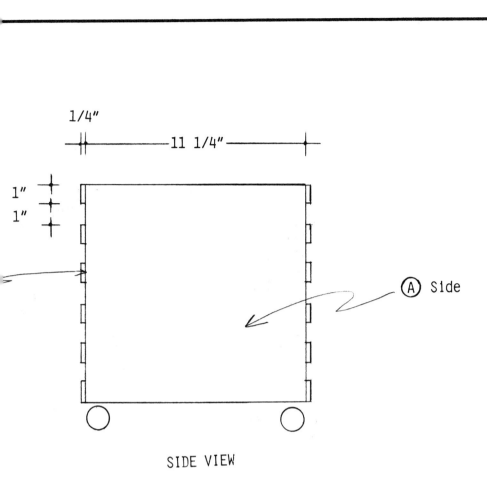

1/4"

11 1/4"

1"

1"

(A) Side

SIDE VIEW

RECORD RACK		
APPROVED BY:		DRAWN BY
DATE: 3/1/83		REVISED
BUILD IT TOGETHER		
Gene and Katie Hamilton		DRAWING NUMBER 23/1

Coat Tree

TIME REQUIRED: almost instant (about two hours; time needed for cutting, building, and assembling project; does not include drying time of glue or finish)

Hang up your coat! That command won't be heard as often in your house once you have one of these dandy coat trees. In a kid's room, a clothes rack like this is a colorful addition that's a lot more likely to be put to use than a hanger in the closet.

We made two, one 4' high, the other 5' high, and painted them in a bright high-gloss enamel. The pole is made of 2″ × 2″ lumber and has four feet made of 1″ × 4″ stock. The hooks are ½″ dowels set into holes drilled into the pole at a slight angle. Inexpensive and easy to make, these coat trees could make a handsome and useful gift.

The 2″ × 2″ lumber may be found at all home centers and lumberyards. Pick carefully through the stack, and choose a good straight piece. You might have to purchase a long two-by-two and have the yardman cut off the warped ends.

You can cut your pole to any length you want. If you are making this clothes rack for one of your apprentices, cut it for a stretching reach, since apprentices grow fast and this tree doesn't.

Cut the ½″ dowel hooks (C) to 5″ lengths, and then lay out their location on the pole. Measure down 3″ from the top of the pole, and make a straight mark across the pole. Then mark the middle of this line (¾″ from edge). This spot is the location of your dowel hole. Duplicate this on the opposite side of the pole. The lower hook is located on an adjacent face of the pole 5″ from the top. Lay it out in the same way on the opposite faces.

We put our hooks in at 20 degrees, but you can angle them as you wish. Mark your angle on a piece of cardboard, and cut it out to act as a guide when you drill.

Clamp the pole to a table, and have one member of the team hold the cardboard guide firmly along the center of the pole. Keep your ½″ drill lined up with the cardboard guide, and all your holes will be drilled at the same angle.

The base pieces (A) for your coat tree are cut two at a time. Measure down the 1″ × 4″ stock 10″. Then mark off a 45-degree angle back toward the end you measured from. Cut along this line to form an angled foot. The angled piece remaining will form the next foot. Cut the next base by measuring over 10″ from the point and make a square cut. Repeat this process to cut the other base.

Drive three number 4 finishing nails into one base piece about 1″ from the square end. Then put glue on one side of pole, put the foot in place flush with the bottom and the side of the pole, and nail it into place. Turn the pole, and glue and nail on the next base and then the next. You will have to move the pole past the end of the table so that the base can drop down for the gluing and nailing of the fourth and the last base.

Your dowel hooks (C) go in quickly. Place glue on the ends and sides of dowels and push them into the holes. After the glue has dried, sand the pole and base smooth and give your tree several coats of paint.

SHOPPING LIST

Item	Quantity
2″ × 2″ pine	5′
1″ × 4″ pine	4′
½″ hardwood dowel	2′
wood glue	6-ounce bottle
number 4 finishing nails	small box
number 120 sandpaper	2 sheets
paint	1 pint
cardboard	

CUTTING LIST

Part	Name	Quantity	Size	Material
A	base	4	¾″ × 3½″ × 10″	1″ × 4″ pine
B	pole	1	1½″ × 1½″ × 4′ or 5′	2″ × 2″ pine
C	dowel hooks	4	½″ × 5″	½″ hardwood dowel

Use a combination square to lay out the position of the lower dowel hook 5″ from the top of the pole.

Hold the cardboard guide at your desired angle along the center of the pole to guide the drill.

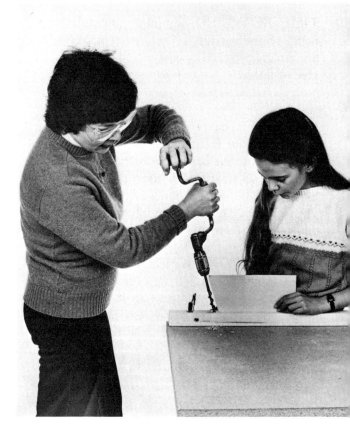

Apply glue to the base pieces (A), and nail them flush with the bottom and even with the back of the pole.

Apply glue to the ends and sides of the dowels (C), and push them into the holes with a twisting motion.

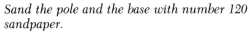

Sand the pole and the base with number 120 sandpaper.

Finished coat tree.

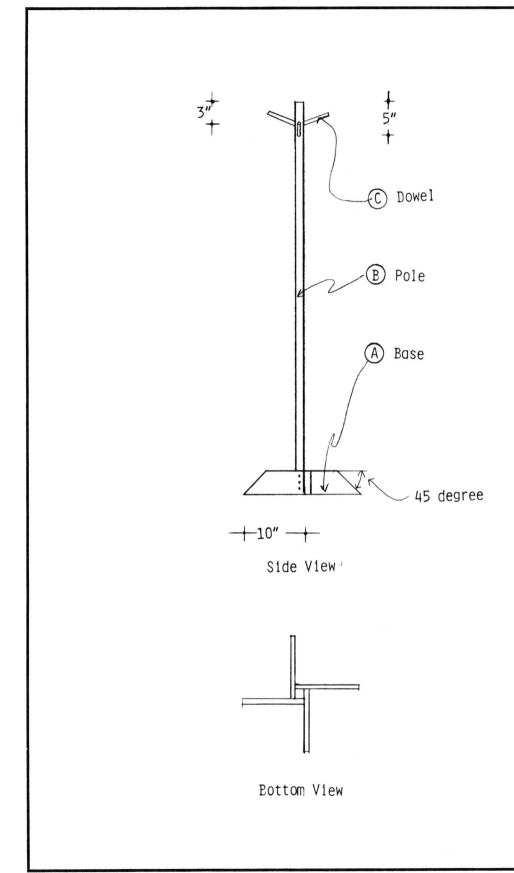

3"   5"

C Dowel

B Pole

A Base

45 degree

10"

Side View

Bottom View

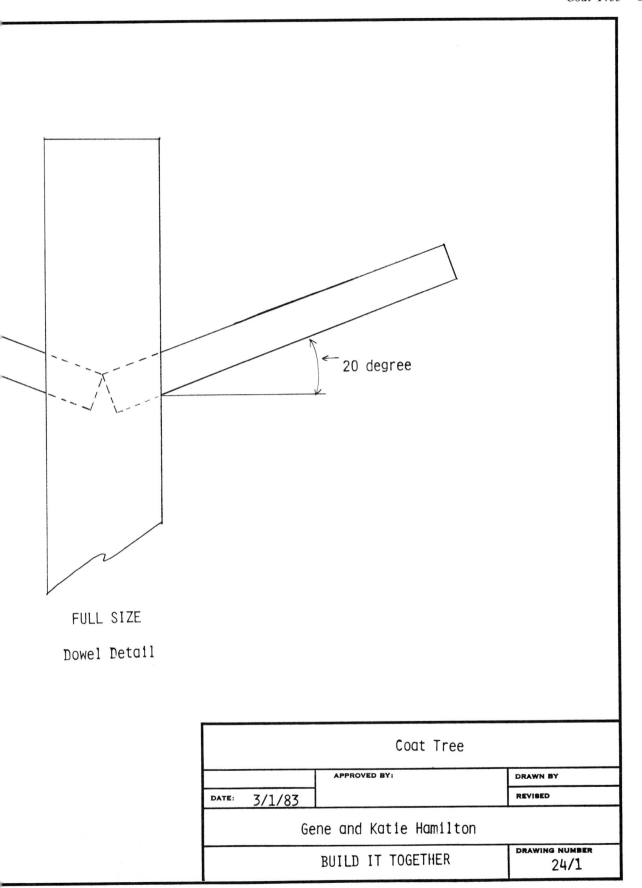

20 degree

FULL SIZE

Dowel Detail

Coat Tree		
	APPROVED BY:	DRAWN BY
DATE: 3/1/83		REVISED
Gene and Katie Hamilton		
BUILD IT TOGETHER		DRAWING NUMBER 24/1

Workbench

TIME REQUIRED: ¾ day (time needed for cutting, building, and assembling project; does not include drying time of glue or finish)

Here's a full-scale workbench for the apprentice, just the right height for the junior partner of a carpentry team. We used 24″-wide flakeboard shelving for the top; the legs are made of sturdy two-by-threes. Flakeboard is inexpensive and will stand up to hard use. It can be easily replaced when too many holes are drilled through the bench top.

A backsplash of one-by-fours frames the top, keeping tools on the bench top. We added a clamp-on woodworking vise.

To make the top (A), your local lumberyard will cut a quarter sheet of flakeboard for you if they do not stock shelving 24″ wide. All the remaining pieces (B, C, D, E, F, G, and H) are cut from dimensional lumber. Lay them out, and cut to length according to measurements on the Cutting List. Use a miter box for square end cuts.

The legs (E) and sides (C) are assembled first. Drive a number 4 box nail into the center of a side piece (C) 1¾″ from its end. Place four more nails

in a box pattern around this central nail. Do the same at the other end of the side, and then put glue on the top 3″ of two legs.

Align the side flush with the top of the leg and even with its inside face. One member of your team should use a square to check that the leg and side are square to one another. The other should do the nailing.

To locate the lower side piece, measure 18″ down from the bottom edge of each side, and mark a line across both legs. Nail up the sides as before, applying a 3″ band of glue to the legs below the layout line. Then align the sides with your lines, using a square to check position, and nail them into place. Check all four legs to see that they are square with the sides, and then drive the other nails home.

Glue and assemble the other leg and side unit, and then, turning the units to rest on the outside of their front legs, place them opposite one another, about 40″ apart, on a flat surface. Drive three nails ¾″ from the ends of the bottom stretcher (D). (Note that this stretcher is 38½″ long and goes inside the side pieces.) Then put glue on the back of the legs where they will come into contact with the bottom stretcher. Put the bottom stretcher in place, butting

173

it against the side, and nail it to the back of the leg. Have one team member hold the leg and side unit upright while his partner nails the bottom stretcher to it.

Drive nails into the ends of one of the other bottom stretchers (B). Then glue and nail it to the outside face of the back legs, even and flush with the lower sides. Glue and nail the second B stretcher to the top of the leg unit, even with upper side piece.

Turn your frame over, and glue and nail on the third B stretcher to the top front of the legs, even with the side pieces. Then turn the frame upright, and glue and nail in the center brace (C). It is located on the top stretcher, 20″ from either side.

Check to see that all the legs are touching the floor. If they are not, see whether your floor is level, or try twisting the frame until all the legs rest on the floor. Be sure to place the frame on a level surface while the glue is drying because it is impossible to straighten the frame after it sets.

All that remains is to lay out the pilot holes in the bench top. Measure 5½″ in from the end of the top (A), and mark a straight line across it. Then measure along this line to the center of the top 12″ from either the front or the back. Mark this point on the top. Then, from this center point, measure 5″ toward the front and 5″ toward the back of the top, and mark these spots. Lay out the other side in the same way, and then drill a ¼″ hole through these points.

Lay out the pilot holes on the cleat (H) in the same manner. Draw a line down the center of the edge of the cleat by measuring ¾″ in from either side. Then make a mark in the center of the cleat 7⅛″ from either end. Drill an ⅛″ hole through this point and on the other cleat. You only have to drill one pilot hole in the cleat; the other two are drilled after it is in place.

Have one of the team members hold the cleat underneath the bench top while the other screws it in place with a number 8 × 2″ wood screw placed in the center hole. Install the other cleat, and then put the top in place. Drill through top pilot holes into the cleat with your ⅛″ drill to make pilot holes, and then insert screws and tighten.

Glue and nail with number 4 finishing nails the backsplash (G) along the back edge flush with the ends of the bench top. Then glue and nail on the ends (F), placing them flush with the back edge of the backsplash.

The top is held in place by two ⅜″ bolts on each side. Drill a ⅜″ pilot hole for these bolts through the side into the cleat. Locate these holes 1½″ down from the top and 4½″ in from the front and back of the frame.

That's it. Your bench is ready for heavy use. We gave our frame a coat of clear sealer and the top two coats of polyurethane varnish. The clamp-on vise is made to be installed on the end of the bench.

SHOPPING LIST

Item	Quantity
¾″ flakeboard	¼ sheet (24″ × 48″)
1″ × 4″ × 8′ pine	4
2″ × 3″ × 8′ pine	2
number 4 box nails	small
number 8 × 2″ wood screw	6
⅜″ × 3″ bolts, nuts, washers	4
wood glue	6 ounce
number 120 sandpaper	2 sheets
finish	1 quart

CUTTING LIST

Part	Name	Quantity	Size	Material
A	top	1	¾″ × 24″ × 48″	flakeboard
B	top stretcher	3	¾″ × 3½″ × 40″	1″ × 4″ pine
C	side/brace	5	¾″ × 3½″ × 19½″	1″ × 4″ pine
D	bottom stretcher	1	¾″ × 3½″ × 38½″	1″ × 4″ pine
E	leg	4	1½″ × 2½″ × 29¼″	2″ × 3″ pine
F	end	2	¾″ × 3½″ × 12″	1″ × 4″ pine
G	backsplash	1	¾″ × 3½″ × 48″	1″ × 4″ pine
H	cleat	2	1½″ × 2½″ × 14½″	2″ × 3″ pine

Drive four number 4 box nails into the ends of the sides (C) around a nail set in the center. Apply glue to the top 3″ of the legs (E).

Use a square to help align the legs and sides while nailing.

Turn the leg and side unit so that it rests on the outside of the back leg. When gluing and nailing the bottom stretcher (D) to the back of the legs, keep it tight against the side and square to the leg.

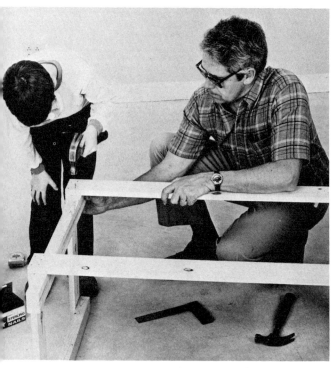

When attaching the top stretcher (B) to the leg and side unit, keep the stretcher even with the end and square with the leg.

Drill a ¼″ pilot hole through the center layout mark. Use the point of a nail set to make a starting hole in the flakeboard for the drill point.

Draw a line 5½″ from the end and straight across the top.

Drill a ⅛″ pilot hole through the center layout mark on the cleat.

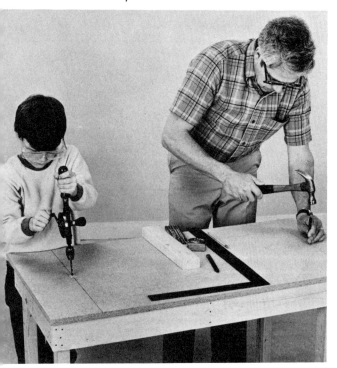

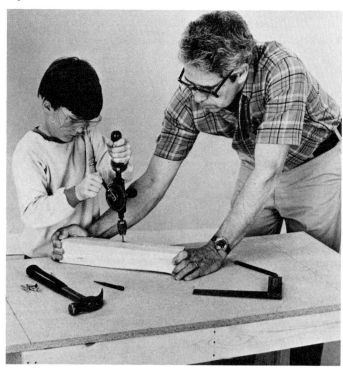

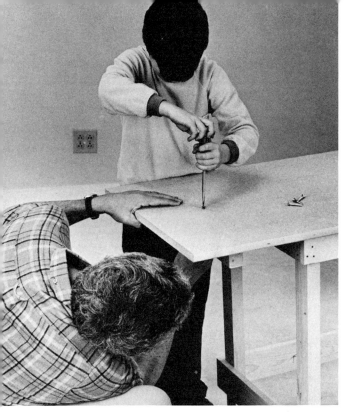

Hold the cleat (H) in place while the center screw is tightened from above.

Glue and nail on the end (F) to the edge of the bench top with number 4 finishing nails.

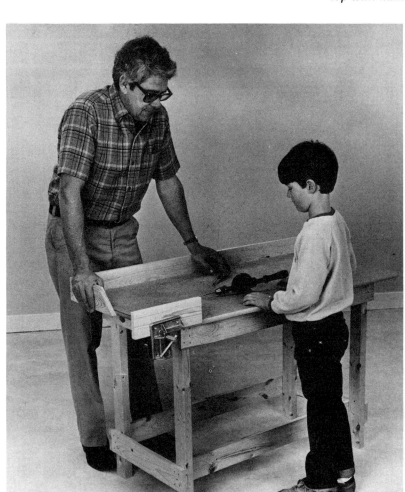

Finished workbench.

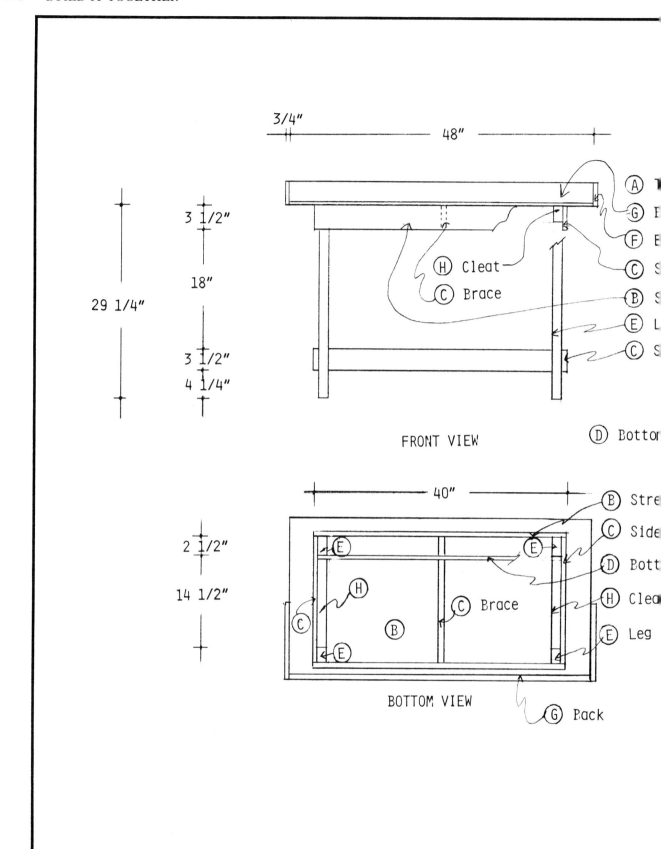

3/4"

48"

3 1/2"

18"

29 1/4"

3 1/2"

4 1/4"

Ⓐ T
Ⓖ E
Ⓕ E
Ⓒ S
Ⓗ Cleat
Ⓒ Brace
Ⓑ S
Ⓔ L
Ⓒ S

FRONT VIEW

Ⓓ Botto

40"

2 1/2"

14 1/2"

Ⓑ Stre
Ⓒ Side
Ⓓ Bott
Ⓗ Clea
Ⓔ Leg

Ⓔ
Ⓗ
Ⓒ
Ⓒ Brace
Ⓑ
Ⓔ

BOTTOM VIEW

Ⓖ Back

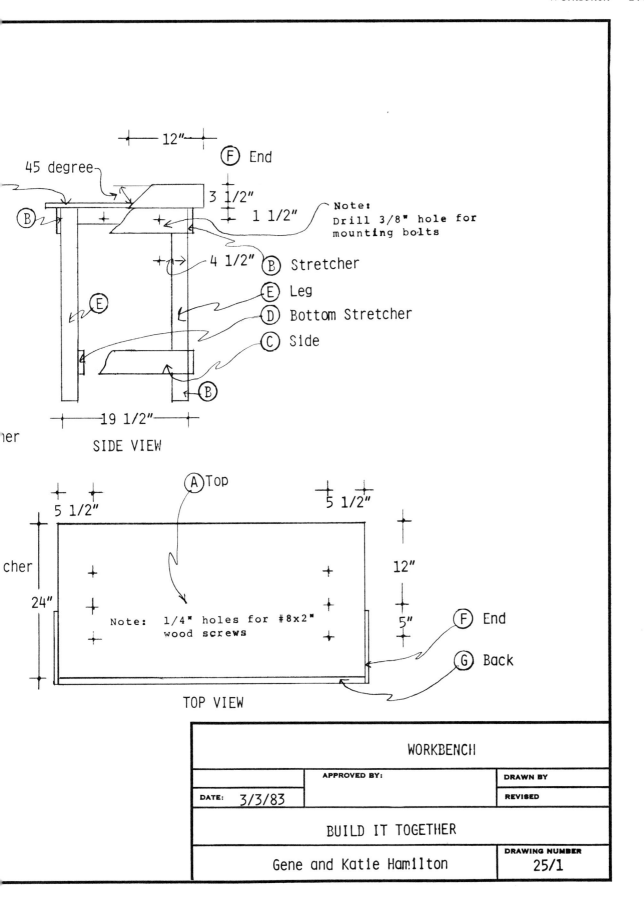

45 degree

12"

(F) End

3 1/2"
1 1/2"

Note:
Drill 3/8" hole for
mounting bolts

(B)

(B) Stretcher

4 1/2"

(E) Leg

(E)

(D) Bottom Stretcher

(C) Side

(B)

19 1/2"

SIDE VIEW

(A) Top

5 1/2"   5 1/2"

12"

Note: 1/4" holes for #8x2"
       wood screws

24"

5"

(F) End

(G) Back

TOP VIEW

WORKBENCH		
	APPROVED BY:	DRAWN BY
DATE: 3/3/83		REVISED
BUILD IT TOGETHER		
Gene and Katie Hamilton		DRAWING NUMBER 25/1

LAUREN

ROBIN

Name Sign

TIME REQUIRED: half day (time needed for cutting, building, and assembling project; does not include drying time of glue or finish)

Just for you, a personalized name board you can hang on your bedroom door or wall. The boards can be made in a variety of ways. Here are two different versions that you can easily make.

Name sign 1 hangs horizontally. It is cut from an inexpensive piece of 1″ × 8″ pine. Trim molding is glued to its face, giving it a frame. The letters are wood, 4″ tall; they are available in home centers and lumberyards. Several coats of spray paint decorate the sign board.

Name sign 2 reads vertically. It is cut from a 1″ × 6″ pine board. The top and bottom corners are cut to an angle, and the wood is finished naturally. For trim we chose a brightly colored ribbon glued onto the outside edge. The sign hangs from a decorative bracket on the top.

Both signs are constructed in the same manner. Measure out the sign board (A), following dimensions on the Cutting List for the name sign

you have chosen. Sign 1 has square corners, but sign 2 has corners cut at a 45-degree angle. To lay these cuts out, measure 1¼″ from the end on both edges of the corner, and mark. Draw a diagonal line connecting these points. Cut along this line to make the angled ends.

Sign 1 is trimmed with decorative molding. Cut the long and short trim (B) and (C) to length using a miter box for accuracy. If the pieces come out a little short, don't worry. However, it is important that parts B and C both be the same length. Because the trim is hardwood, pilot holes must be drilled for the nails so that the wood won't split. Better let the older carpenter drill the holes, because the ⁄₁₆″ bit needed for this breaks easily. Drill two holes about 1½″ from the ends of part C. Then drill holes 1½″ from the ends of part B and in its center. These nails will hold the molding in place while the glue dries. Attach the molding to name sign 1 with wood glue and small finishing nails. Wipe off any excess glue with a rag while it is wet.

Name sign 2 has ribbon trim around its sides attached with wood glue. We choose a red and white decorative ribbon ¾″ wide. Apply the glue sparingly to the sides, top, and bottom of the sign so it doesn't soak through and stain the ribbon.

Both signs have the same precut wooden letters. Use spray paint to color them. Several coats will be necessary, so use plenty of newspaper to protect your table. Open a window for proper ventilation, and don't paint in the basement near a hot water heater or other open flame because mist from a spray can is highly inflammable.

When the paint has dried, use small finishing nails to hold the letters in place. The older team member should supervise placement.

Hanging brackets go on next. Sign 1 uses a back-mounted picture-hanging bracket (E). Nail it in place with the brads that come with the bracket. Hammer carefully, checking that the nails don't go all the way through the board.

Sign 2 is held up by a decorative hanger (E) that screws into the top of the sign. Make a pilot hole for the screw by gently driving a finishing nail partway into the top and then removing it. Screw the hanger into this hole.

SHOPPING LIST FOR NAME SIGN 1

Item	Quantity
1″ × 8″ pine	2′
¼″ hardwood decorative molding	7′
4″ precut letters	as needed
medium-sized picture hanger	1
wood glue	6-ounce bottle
number 120 sandpaper	2 sheets
spray paint	1 can

CUTTING LIST FOR NAME SIGN 1

Part	Name	Quantity	Size	Material
A	sign board	1	¾″ × 7¼″ × 24″	1 × 8 pine
B	long trim	2	¼″ × ½″ × 23¼″	trim molding
C	short trim	2	¼″ × ½″ × 6¾″	trim molding

SHOPPING LIST FOR NAME SIGN 2

Item	Quantity
1″ × 6″ pine	3′
¾″ ribbon	6′
4″ precut letters	as needed
decorative picture-hanging bracket	1
wood glue	6-ounce bottle
number 120 sandpaper	2 sheets
spray paint	1 can

CUTTING LIST FOR NAME SIGN 2

Part	Name	Quantity	Size	Material
A	sign board	1	¾″ × 5½″ × 29½″	1″ × 6″ pine
B	ribbon trim	1	¾″ × 6′	decorative ribbon

To make the angled corners on name sign 2, measure
1¼″ along the edge of the sign in both directions.

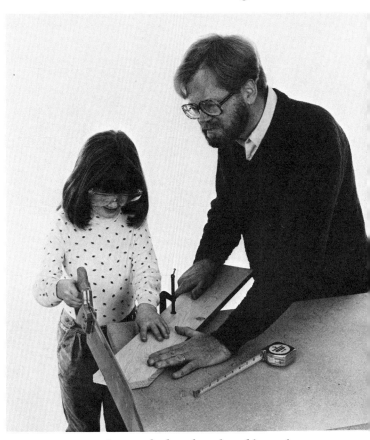

Secure the board to the table, and
then cut the corners off at a 45-
degree angle.

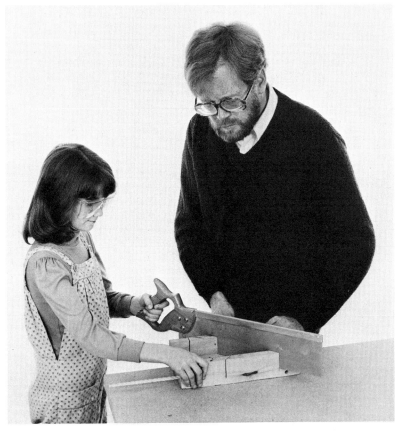

Cut trim B and C for name sign 1 in a
miter box to ensure having a 45-degree
corner.

Drill pilot holes in the molding with a ⅟₁₆″ drill.

Apply glue to the molding.

Nail the molding in place about ½″ from the edge. Carefully align it so that the corners are square.

Cover a table with paper, and set the letters on a piece of scrap wood. Paint in a room that has proper ventilation.

The letters are nailed into place with small finishing nails. The ribbon trim for sign 2 is glued to the edge with wood glue.

Attach the hanging bracket to the back of sign 1. The decorative hanger is screwed into the top of sign 2.

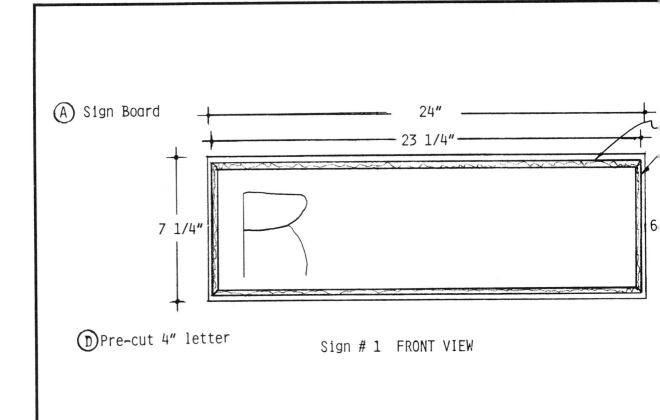

(A) Sign Board

24"

23 1/4"

7 1/4"

6

(D) Pre-cut 4" letter

Sign # 1   FRONT VIEW

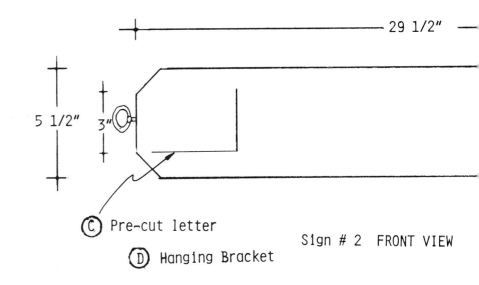

29 1/2"

5 1/2"   3"

(C) Pre-cut letter

(D) Hanging Bracket

Sign # 2   FRONT VIEW

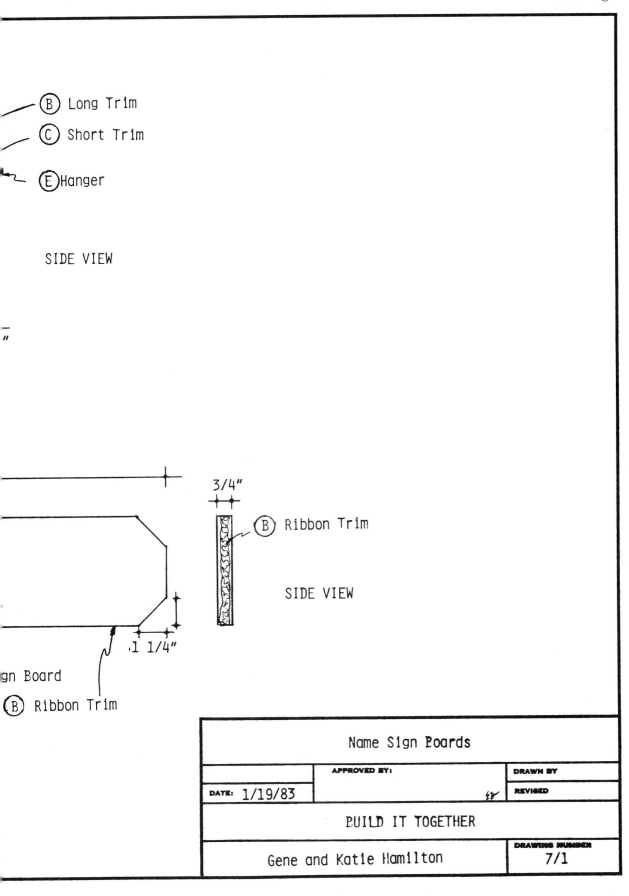

(B) Long Trim

(C) Short Trim

(E) Hanger

SIDE VIEW

"

3/4"

(B) Ribbon Trim

SIDE VIEW

1 1/4"

gn Board

(B) Ribbon Trim

Name Sign Boards		
	APPROVED BY:	DRAWN BY
DATE: 1/19/83		REVISED
BUILD IT TOGETHER		
Gene and Katie Hamilton		DRAWING NUMBER 7/1

Elevated Play Fort

TIME REQUIRED: weekend (time needed for cutting, building, and assembling project; does not include drying time for glue and finish)

This easy-to-construct play fort is likely to be labeled "off limits" to adults after it's built. The fort will surely become a special retreat for the girl or boy who can take title to it, but during the weekend of construction, teamwork will be needed. The fort can be located in any corner of the yard. In fact, since it is raised, it can even go over an existing sandbox or other play area.

If the construction team is ambitious, the fort can be a foundation for expansion. The lower area might be enclosed, walls and a doorway could be added, and a wood roof or tarpaulin might be attached. Only your imagination sets the limit.

The basic module of the fort is a 7'-square raised platform made of 4" × 4" pressure-treated wood corner posts embedded firmly in the ground or in cement. Only safe, easy-to-use hand tools are needed to complete the fort, although a circular power saw will speed the cutting. A post-hole digger, which can be rented, is also helpful.

Construction grade two-by-sixes and two-by-fours are used for the joists and decking; stock-cut closet poll create the ladder rungs. Nails are the only hardware required. The fort is protected from the elements with either paint or stain.

Choosing and loading the materials at the lumberyard, selecting the site, cutting the wood, positioning and nailing everything together, and, of course, cleaning up while the finish dries all require team effort. While cutting wood is probably best tackled by the adult team member, there's measuring and nailing aplenty to keep all hands busy. Wear work gloves for protection from splintering wood and safety glasses when cutting or nailing lumber.

After you've chosen the site for your fort, shop for the materials and assemble your tools. Site layout is the first job. To lay out the square for the fort, use the simple string technique to locate each post. Pick out four short pieces of scrap wood for stakes, and drive one into the ground where the first leg of your fort will be. Tie string around this stake and stretch it diagonally 9' to the place where you want the opposite post to be. Drive a second temporary stake there. With the string still tied to the first post, stretch it at right angles 6½' to the

189

place where you think the third corner post will be. At the same time have your helper tie and stretch a string 6½' from the second post to the stake you are holding. Where these two strings meet is the approximate location of the third post.

Do the same on the other side, and you will have the four corners laid out. Check to see that the measurement from corner to opposite corner is approximately 9' and adjust accordingly.

Here's where the post-hole digger is helpful. Dig the post holes oversize to allow movement of the post into exact position when nailing on the header (B) and the joists (C).

Excavate the post holes to a depth of at least a foot, and fill the bottom of each hole with several inches of crushed stone. Place a post in the hole on the lowest part of the site and temporarily nail a couple of two-by-fours to the post to brace it while you and your helper plumb (adjust it until vertical) it with a level. While your helper holds the post vertical, drive a stake into the ground next to the two-by-four and then nail the two-by-four to the stake. Do the same to the other brace.

Next, install a post adjacent to the first post. Brace it in place, and then measure from the ground up (approximately 4') to where you want the deck of the fort to be. Make a level mark on the post here.

Cut the two headers (B) to 7' and the four joists (C) to 6' 9". Then have one team member hold up one end of a header while the other temporarily nails it to the post, level with the mark and flush with the side of the post. Use a single nail, and don't sink the head. Place a level on the header, and have one team member watch it as the other nails the other end of the header in place on the first post.

Place the next post in the hole adjacent to the first post, and repeat the leveling, this time using a joist (C). Nail the joist to the inside of the corner posts. Check the corner to be sure that it's square, and adjust the position of one of the posts if it isn't. Then place the fourth post in position, and stretch the header and joist to it.

Plumb up the posts with the level. You might have to dig the holes slightly larger to move the base of the posts. Keep working from post to post until they are all plumb and the joists and headers are level.

When everything is square, nail each header

and joist to the post with four additional number 16 galvanized common nails. Then replace the dirt around the posts, packing it in tightly. The fort is stable enough to be freestanding, but cement in the post holes; it will protect the legs from rot.

The 2 center joists are installed next. Measure 24" in from each of the outside joists, and mark these points on the header. Nail the joist in place at these points with four number 16 galvanized nails. Have one team member keep them square while the other does the nailing.

Now that the framework is complete, the ladder is constructed. Place the remaining post in position 18" from the front corner post on the side where you want the ladder. Bounce it on the ground to make a depression, and then dig a shallow hole where this mark is. Place the post back in position, and plumb it with the level. While one member holds it, the other should temporarily nail it in place with a single nail driven through the back side of the joist into the post.

Lay out the first ladder rung on the face of the posts. Have one member place the level even with the joist and keep it leveled while the other marks this position on both posts. Measure down a foot and keep repeating this process until you are at the lowest rung, which should be less than a foot from the ground.

Remove the post, and transfer the lines from the face to the side with a combination square. Drill a 1½"-deep 1¼" hole for each rung. Do the same on the upright post.

Cut the rungs out of the hardwood dowels to a length of 21". Then assemble the rungs in the stationary post, and fit them into the inside post. To seat the rungs in the holes, use a hammer to hit a piece of scrap placed against the post for protection. When the rungs are fully seated in their holes and level, nail the center post in position by driving number 16 galvanized common nails through the rear of the joist. Replace the dirt in the inside post hole.

Your fort will take shape fast now that the hard work is done. Have one team member measure the twenty-one pieces of 2" × 4" decking (D) to 7' while the other cuts it to length. Notch the outside decking pieces to fit around the corner posts. The decking will also have to be cut flush with the joist in the area of the ladder for hand clearance.

Use a piece of ¼″-thick wood placed between the decking pieces to keep the spacing even. Work as a team from each end. Put the spacer in place, slide the decking tight against it and align it even on the ends, and then drive one nail home. As you position the last pieces, adjust the spacing visually.

When you both have finished single nailing all the decking, add another nail to the ends and two nails along each of the center joists.

The railings are installed next. It is easier to nail the whole two-by-four in place and then cut the end off. Begin by measuring 36″ up from the deck of the fort, marking this point on each post. Put a side rail in place, and nail it so that the end is flush with the side of the post. Cut the other end flush. Install the other top side rails, and then go on to the lower side rails, which are nailed midway between the deck and top rail, about 14″ down. Add the front and back bottom rails, cutting these flush with the outside of the top side rail.

The posts can now be cut flush with the top rail. If one sticks up higher than the rest because of your sloping lot, use it as a flagpole.

The sway braces are cut in pairs. The front and rear sets attach to the outside face of the joist and the back side of the post. Those for the sides are nailed to the underside of the header and the outside face of the post. Try each set before you nail everything together. Drive the nails at an angle, since the number 16 nails are longer than the thickness of two two-by-fours. Check to see whether any nails protrude, and bend their points over with your hammer if they do.

The only job left is protecting the fort from the elements. Latex stain is the easiest to apply. Use an inexpensive brush and purchase a ½″ nap roller cover for the flat areas. When you are finished, throw the roller away.

SHOPPING LIST

Item	Quantity
4″ × 4″ × 10′ pine	6
2″ × 6″ × 8′ pine	10
2″ × 4″ × 8′ pine	36
1¼″ × 6′ closet poll	1
number 16 galvanized common nails	1 box
wood stain	1 gallon
crushed stone	1 bushel

CUTTING LIST

Part	Name	Quantity	Size	Material
A	post	5	10′	4″ × 4″ pine
B	header	2	7′	2″ × 6″ pine
C	joist	4	6′ 9″	2″ × 6″ pine
D	decking	21	7′	2″ × 4″ pine
E	side rail	6	6′ 9″	2″ × 4″ pine
F	front rail	8	6′ 6″	2″ × 4″ pine
L	ladder rung	6	cut to fit	1¼″ closet poll

Lay out the base of the fort by driving stakes into the ground to form a 6½′ square. Adjust the stakes until the distance from opposite corners is equal.

Use a level when installing the headers (B) and joists (C). Start at the lowest post, and work from post to post.

Insert a post (A) into the hole on the lowest area of the site, and plumb it with a level. Use two-by-fours as braces to hold the post in place.

Nail the center two joists in place 24″ from each end of the joists. Hold it straight, and use four number 16 galvanized common nails.

Mark the location of the ladder rungs on a corner post. With a level, transfer these locations to the inside ladder post.

Lay the inside ladder post on the ground, and drill the rung holes.

When the rungs are level, nail the inside ladder post to the joist with four number 16 galvanized nails driven through the joist from underneath the fort.

Measure and cut the decking (D) to a length of 7′. Nail the decking pieces in place with number 16 galvanized nails.

Use a piece of ¼″-thick scrap wood as a spacer when nailing the decking in place.

Notch the outside decking pieces to accommodate the corner posts and inside ladder post.

Nail the top rails in place 36″ above the decking. First place the side rails and then the front and rear rails.

Use a handsaw to trim the rails even with the corner posts.

Cut the corner posts and ladder post even with the rails.

Finished elevated play fort.

Cut and install the corner bracing pairs. Nail the front and rear brace to the outside of the joist and inside of the post. Do the opposite for the side braces.

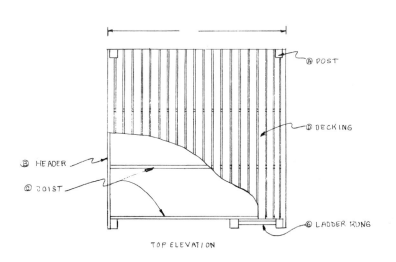

Ⓐ POST

Ⓓ DECKING

Ⓑ HEADER

Ⓒ JOIST

Ⓖ LADDER RUNG

TOP ELEVATION

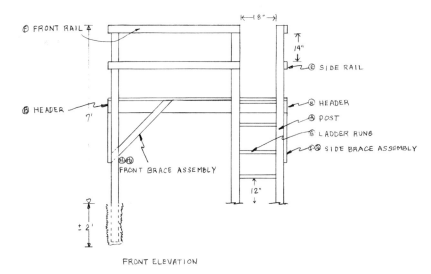

Ⓕ FRONT RAIL

8"

14"

Ⓔ SIDE RAIL

Ⓑ HEADER

7'

Ⓑ HEADER

Ⓐ POST

Ⓖ LADDER RUNG

Ⓘ⊘ SIDE BRACE ASSEMBLY

Ⓗ⊕ⓗ

FRONT BRACE ASSEMBLY

12"

± 2'

FRONT ELEVATION

18X24   PRINTED ON NO. 1000H CLEARPRINT

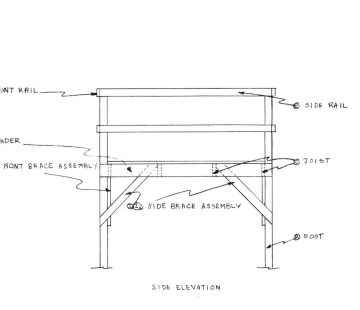

NT RAIL

ⒺSIDE RAIL

DER

RONT BRACE ASSEMBLY

ⒸJOIST

ⒾⒿ SIDE BRACE ASSEMBLY

ⒶPOST

SIDE ELEVATION

PART IDENTIFICATION

NAME	MATERIAL
Ⓐ POST	4×4
Ⓑ HEADER	2×6
Ⓒ JOIST	2×6
Ⓓ DECKING	2×4
Ⓔ SIDE RAIL	2×4
Ⓕ FRONT RAIL	2×4
Ⓖ LADDER RUNG	CLOSET POLE 1¼" DIAMETER
Ⓗ FRONT BRACE	2×4
Ⓗ₁ FRONT BRACE	2×4
Ⓘ SIDE BRACE	2×4
Ⓙ SIDE BRACE	2×4

ⒾSIDE BRACE   Ⓙ SIDE BRACE

ⒽFRONT BRACE   Ⓗ FRONT BRACE

BRACE DETAIL

NOTE: #16 GALVANIZED COMMON NAILS USED
FOR FRAMING AND DECKING

ALL LUMBER DIMENSIONS NOMINAL

ELEVATED PLAY FORT "BUILD IT TOGETHER"	2×		
	APPROVED BY:		DRAWN BY E.C.H.
DATE:			REVISED
			DRAWING NUMBER